The Impact of the Dead Sea Scrolls

Joseph A. Fitzmyer, S.J.

Paulist Press
New York/Mahwah, NJ

Cover photo and photos on pp. 3, 10, 17, 20, 25, 52, and 134 by Michael Kerrigan, CSP. Photos and illustrations on pp. 39, 59, 63, and 130 from Paulist Press Archive Collection.

Cover design by Sharyn Banks
Book design by Lynn Else

Library of Congress Cataloging-in-Publication Data

Fitzmyer, Joseph A.
   The impact of the Dead Sea scrolls / Joseph A. Fitzmyer.
     p. cm.
   Includes bibliographical references and index.
   ISBN 978-0-8091-4615-4 (alk. paper)
   1. Dead Sea scrolls. 2. Qumran community. 3. Dead Sea scrolls—Relation to the New Testament. I. Title.
   BM487.F546 2009
   296.1'55—dc22

                               2009016043

Published by Paulist Press
997 Macarthur Boulevard
Mahwah, New Jersey 07430

www.paulistpress.com

Printed and bound in the
United States of America

CONTENTS

Contents

PREFACE

Now that the vast majority of the Dead Sea Scrolls have been published either in individual volumes or in the official series put out by the Clarendon Press of Oxford, the time has come for an assessment of the impact that the scrolls have made. Almost a quarter of the scrolls preserve parts of the Hebrew Bible, and they have revealed much about the reliability of the Masoretic Text (the text of medieval tradition found in the current Hebrew Bible). Some of these biblical texts are very old, having been copied even before the members of the Jewish sect settled at Qumran, to which they brought them. Many other scrolls are sectarian compositions, that is, writings that describe the life of such ancient Jews who lived at Qumran. Most of the scrolls were written in Hebrew, but a few also in Aramaic. In one instance, the text is preserved in both Hebrew and Aramaic (the deuterocanonical Book of Tobit). Moreover, all the scrolls, biblical, sectarian, and parabiblical literary compositions provide an ancient Palestinian background for the Christian Gospels and other New Testament writings. Hence the Dead Sea Scrolls have influenced not only the study of the Old Testament or the Hebrew Scriptures, but also the history of Judaism in Judea, the study of the ancient languages of Aramaic and Hebrew, and the interpretation of many New Testament writings.

Most of the scrolls, unfortunately, are fragmentary, but many of these are large fragments, and a few are almost complete texts. Though such fragmentary writings supply one with important information, the missing lines and words prevent one from deriving the full story from them. And yet, one can learn from them what constitutes the impact that the Dead Sea Scrolls have made in human intellectual life. This impact is the purpose of my writing.

I have to thank the Rev. J. Leon Hooper, S.J., director of the Woodstock Theological Center Library, and the members of his staff, for the help that they have provided in getting needed books for my use.

The schematic plan of Khirbet Qumran reproduced in this book on page xii is derived from plate XXXIX of the book by R. de Vaux, O.P., *Archaelogy and the Dead Sea Scrolls*, published by Oxford University Press, Oxford, UK, and is used with the permission of that Press and of the British Academy, for which the Press published that book.

Joseph A. Fitzmyer, S.J.

ABBREVIATIONS

1. General

AB	Anchor Bible
Ag.Ap.	Josephus, *Against Apion*
Ant.	Josephus, *Antiquities of the Jews*
BARev	*Biblical Archaeology Review*
BETL	Bibliotheca Ephemeridum Theologicarum Lovaniensium
Bib	*Biblica*
BibOr	Biblica et Orientalia
BRev	*Bible Review*
CBQ	*Catholic Biblical Quarterly*
DJD	Discoveries in the Judaean Desert
DSD	*Dead Sea Discoveries*
Eccles. Hist.	Eusebius, *Ecclesiastical History*
ErIsr	Eretz Israel
ESBNT	J. A. Fitzmyer, *Essays on the Semitic Background of the New Testament* (London: Chapman, 1971); see also *SBNT*
IEJ	*Israel Exploration Journal*
JBL	*Journal of Biblical Literature*
JJS	*Journal of Jewish Studies*
JQR	*Jewish Quarterly Review*
JSNT	*Journal for the Study of the New Testament*
JSNTSup	Supplements to *JSNT*
JSP	*Journal for the Study of the Pseudepigrapha*
JSPSup	Supplements to *JSP*
J.W.	Josephus, *Jewish War*
Nat. Hist.	Pliny the Elder, *Naturalis historia*
NT	New Testament
NTOA	Novum Testamentum et Orbis Antiquus

OT   Old Testament
QL   Qumran Literature
RB   *Revue Biblique*
RevQ   *Revue de Qumran*
SBNT   J. A. Fitzmyer, *The Semitic Background of the New Testament* (Grand Rapids: Eerdmans; Livonia, MI: Dove Booksellers, 1997)
SBT   Studies in Biblical Theology
SDSSRL   Studies in the Dead Sea Scrolls and Related Literature
TS   *Theological Studies*

2. Dead Sea Scrolls

CD   Damascus Document of Cairo
1QapGen   Genesis Apocryphon of Qumran Cave 1
lQDan   Daniel of Qumran Cave 1
1QEnGiants   Enoch Giants of Qumran Cave 1
1QH   *Hodayot* (Thanksgiving Psalms) of Qumran Cave 1
1QInstruction   Instruction (Sapiential text) of Qumran Cave 1
lQIsa^a First copy of Isaiah of Qumran Cave 1
1QIsa^b Second copy of Isaiah of Qumran Cave 1
lQJub   *Jubilees* of Qumran Cave 1
1QM   War Scroll of Qumran Cave 1
1QNJ   New Jerusalem of Qumran Cave 1
1QpHab   Pesher of Habakkuk of Qumran Cave 1
1QpMic   Pesher of Micah of Qumran Cave 1
1QpPs   Pesher of Psalms of Qumran Cave 1
1QpZeph   Pesher of Zephaniah of Qumran Cave 1
1QS   *Serek hayyahad* (Manual of Discipline) of Qumran Cave 1
1QSa   Rule of the Congregation of Qumran Cave 1
1QSb   Collection of Blessings of Qumran Cave 1
2QEnGiants   Enoch Giants of Qumran Cave 2
2QJub   *Jubilees* of Qumran Cave 2
2QNJ   New Jerusalem of Qumran Cave 2

2QSir	Ben Sira of Qumran Cave 2
3QJub	*Jubilees* of Qumran Cave 3
3QpIsa	Pesher of Isaiah of Qumran Cave 3
4QAgesCreat	Ages of Creation of Qumran Cave 4
4QapJosh	Apocryphon of Joshua of Qumran Cave 4
4QApocMess	Messianic Apocalypse of Qumran Cave 4
4QapPent	Apocryphal Pentateuch of Qumran Cave 4
4QBarNaf	Barki Nafshi of Qumran Cave 4
4QBeat	Beatitudes of Qumran Cave 4
4QBer	*Běrākôt* (Blessings) of Qumran Cave 4
4QBirthNoah	Birth of Noah of Qumran Cave 4
4QCalDoc	Calendaric Document of Qumran Cave 4
4QCa1DocM	Calendaric Document/Mishmarot of Qumran Cave 4
4QCatena	Catena of Qumran Cave 4
4QD	Damascus Document of Qumran Cave 4
4QDan	Daniel of Qumran Cave 4
4QDanSuz	Daniel-Suzanna of Qumran Cave 4
4QDeut	Deuteronomy of Qumran Cave 4
4QDibHam	*Dibrê Ham-mě'ôrôt* (Words of the Luminaries) of Qumran Cave 4
4QEn	Enoch of Qumran Cave 4
4QEnastr	Enoch Astronomical Book of Qumran Cave 4
4QEnGiants	Enoch Giants of Qumran Cave 4
4QExod	Exodus of Qumran Cave 4
4QEzra	Ezra of Qumran Cave 4
4QFlor	Florilegium of Qumran Cave 4
4QFourKgdms	Four Kingdoms of Qumran Cave 4
4QHoroscope	Horoscope of Qumran Cave 4
4QInstrCompB	Instruction-like Composition B of Qumran Cave 4
4QInstruction	Instruction (Sapiential text) of Qumran Cave 4
4QJub	*Jubilees* of Qumran Cave 4
4QLXXDeut	Septuagint Deuteronomy of Qumran Cave 4
4QLXXLev	Septuagint Leviticus of Qumran Cave 4
4QLXXNum	Septuagint Numbers of Qumran Cave 4
4QM	War Scroll of Qumran Cave 4
4QMez	Mezuzah of Qumran Cave 4

4QMMT	*Miqṣat maʿaśê hat-tôrāh* (Some Works of the Law) of Qumran Cave 4
4QNoncanPs	Noncanonical Psalms of Qumran Cave 4
4QpaleoDeut	Deuteronomy in paleo-Hebrew script of Qumran Cave 4
4QpaleoGen	Genesis in paleo-Hebrew script of Qumran Cave 4
4QpaleoGenExod	Genesis-Exodus in paleo-Hebrew script of Qumran Cave 4
4QpaleoJob	Job in paleo-Hebrew script of Qumran Cave 4
4QNJ	New Jerusalem of Qumran Cave 4
4QpGen	Pesher of Genesis of Qumran Cave 4
4QpHos	Pesher of Hosea of Qumran Cave 4
4QpIsa	Pesher of Isaiah of Qumran Cave 4
4QpMic	Pesher of Micah of Qumran Cave 4
4QpNah	Pesher of Nahum of Qumran Cave 4
4QpPs	Pesher of Psalms of Qumran Cave 4
4QprNab	Prayer of Nabonidus of Qumran Cave 4
4QpZeph	Pesher of Zephaniah of Qumran Cave 4
4Qphyl	Phylactery of Qumran Cave 4
4QS	Manual of Discipline of Qumran Cave 4
4QSam	Samuel of Qumran Cave 4
4QShirShabb	Shirot Shabbat (Sabbath Songs) of Qumran Cave 4
4QSonofGod	Son of God text of Qumran Cave 4
4QTestim	Testimonia of Qumran Cave 4
4QtgJob	Targum of Job of Qumran Cave 4
4QtgLev	Targum of Leviticus of Qumran Cave 4
4QTob	Tobit of Qumran Cave 4
4QWiles	Wiles of the Wicked Woman of Qumran Cave 4
4QWisText	Wisdom Text of Qumran Cave 4
4QZodBront	Zodiology and Brontology of Qumran Cave 4
pap4QparaKings	Paraphrase of Kings on papyrus of Qumran Cave 4
5QD	Damascus Document of Qumran Cave 5
5QNJ	New Jerusalem of Qumran Cave 5
5QpMal	Pesher of Malachi of Qumran Cave 5

5QS	Manual of Discipline of Qumran Cave 5
6QCalDoc	Calendaric Document of Qumran Cave 6
6QD	Damascus Document of Qumran Cave 6
6QDan	Daniel of Qumran Cave 6
7QEpJer	Epistle of Jeremy of Qumran Cave 7
7QExodus	Exodus of Qumran Cave 7
8QMez	Mezuzah of Qumran Cave 8
11QHymns	Hymns of Qumran Cave 11
11QJub	*Jubilees* of Qumran Cave 11
11QMelch	Melchizedek Text of Qumran Cave 11
11QNJ	New Jerusalem of Qumran Cave 11
11QpaleoLev	Leviticus written in paleo-Hebrew script from Qumran Cave 11
11QPs	Psalms of Qumran Cave 11
11QShirShabb	Shirot Shabbat (Sabbath Songs) of Qumran Cave 11
11QTemple	Temple Scroll of Qumran Cave 11
11QtgJob	Targum of Job of Qumran Cave 11
MasShirShabb	Shirot Shabbat (Sabbath Songs) of Masada

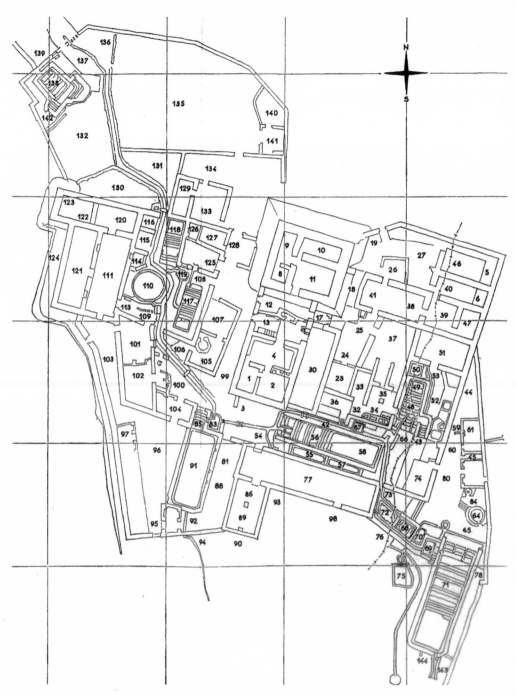

Khirbet Quaran: schematic plan and position of
the loci in Periods I*b* and II.

I

THE DEAD SEA SCROLLS:
Terminology, Discovery, and Dating

Terminology

"Dead Sea Scrolls" is a term used today both in a broad sense and in a narrow sense. In the broad sense, it denotes texts, not discovered in the Dead Sea itself, but in caves and holes along the northwest shore of the Dead Sea between 1947 and 1963. Although a few of these scrolls are complete, the vast majority of them are fragmentary and some are tiny. They are not all related to one another but come from about a dozen sites along that northwest shore. In the broad sense, the term includes texts discovered during the last decade of the nineteenth century in the genizah ("hide-away," for old, worn-out Jewish writings) of the Synagogue of Ezra in Fustat (Old Cairo), Egypt. It also includes writings found in the caves of the Wadi ("torrent-bed") Murabba'at (173 writings), Wadi Khabra (Naḥal Ḥever, 70), Wadi Seiyal (Naḥal Ṣe'elim, 84?), Wadi Mahras (Naḥal Mishmar, 8), Khirbet ("stone-ruin") Mird (Kastellion, 100), 'Ain Ghweir (2), Keteph Jericho (19), Wadi Nar (5), Wadi Sdeir (4), Khirbet Mazin, and at Masada (850?).

In the narrow sense, however, "Dead Sea Scrolls" means the scrolls and fragments retrieved from eleven caves located near the Wadi Qumran at the northwest corner of the Dead Sea, but also texts related to them found elsewhere. These scrolls and fragments number today about 825, and six or seven more from the Cairo genizah are related to them. From Qumran Cave 1 (1Q) came seven manuscripts and 72 fragments; from 2Q: 33 texts; from 3Q: 15 texts; from 4Q: 582? texts; from 5Q: 25 texts; from 6Q: 31 texts; from 7Q: 19 texts (all Greek); from 8Q: five texts; from 9Q: one

1

text; from 10Q: one text; from 11Q: 31 texts; from an unidentified cave: seven texts. Caves 1, 4, and 11 have yielded the most important writings. The rest of the discussion in this book will concentrate on the scrolls in the narrow sense, that is, the Qumran Scrolls and fragments, the so-called Qumran literature (QL). So much for the terminology of the Dead Sea Scrolls.

Discovery

Although we probably shall never learn the full story of the discovery of the Qumran Scrolls, certain details about it are known from the year 1947, when the scrolls came to light for the first time. At that time, the British Mandate of Palestine controlled the area from the Mediterranean Sea to the western shore of the Dead Sea. The State of Israel did not yet exist; it came into being on 14 May 1948, when the Jews living there declared their independence. The first Arab–Jewish War broke out on 15 May and lasted until the cease-fire and truce of 7 January 1949. The Arabs who had been living in the British Mandate then began to occupy the area that came to be known as the West Bank (i.e., of the Jordan River and the Dead Sea), which was controlled by the Hashemite Kingdom of Jordan in the time subsequent to the first Arab–Jewish War. It was in the area of the British Mandate of Palestine that the discovery of scrolls first took place in 1947. Subsequent discoveries were made in the Arab territory of the West Bank.

During 1947, some Bedouin herdsmen of the tribe of Taʿâmireh found the scrolls in what came to be known as Qumran Cave 1, a cave situated about a mile north of Khirbet Qumran, a site that lies about half a mile in from the northwest shore of the Dead Sea. That site had often been regarded as the ruins of a construction dating from Roman times in Palestine, with tombs of a cemetery thought at times to have been related to a Muslim sect.

A Bedouin boy, subsequently identified as Jumʿa Muhammad Khalil, had been tending goats, when one of them went astray. As he went in search of it, he idly tossed a stone through a hole in a cliff and heard it break something. Out of curiosity, he and some companions returned two days later, enlarged the hole, and crept

CAVE 4 AT QUMRAN

into a small cave. There one of the companions, Muhammad ed-Di'b, discovered eight jars, in two of which he found seven scrolls, some wrapped in ancient linen, along with many fragments. In March 1947, he and his companions brought the scrolls and fragments to an antiquities dealer in Bethlehem, known as Kando (Khalil Iskander Shahin).

Kando happened to be a member of the Syrian Orthodox Church, and he told the Metropolitan, Mar Athanasius Yeshue Samuel, the superior of St. Mark's Monastery in the Old City of Jerusalem, about the discovery. Without understanding the value of the scrolls, the Metropolitan bought five of them, which turned out to be four scrolls: a complete copy of Isaiah (1QIsa[a]), the *Pesher* (commentary) on Habakkuk (lQpHab), the Manual of Discipline (1QS [in two parts]), and the Aramaic Genesis Apocryphon (lQapGen). Story has it that those four scrolls cost the Metropolitan the equivalent of only £24 (then equal to about $100).

On 29 November 1947, the date on which the United Nations had resolved to create the State of Israel, Eleazar Lipa Sukenik, a professor at the Hebrew University in Jerusalem, returned from a visit to the United States and learned about the discovery of the scrolls in Cave 1 from an antiquities dealer. Just about the time that the British Mandate was coming to an end, Sukenik managed to get to Bethlehem and secured from the dealer six rolls, which turned out to be three scrolls: an incomplete copy of Isaiah (lQIsa^b), the *Hodayot* (Thanksgiving Psalms [in four parts]), and the War Scroll (1QM). Subsequently Sukenik learned about the purchase of the four scrolls by the Metropolitan and tried to visit St. Mark's Monastery, unsuccessfully, because of the unsettled political situation in Jerusalem at that time. Toward the end of January 1948, however, Sukenik managed to visit the Metropolitan in a certain military zone and to borrow the scrolls from him for three days. He then copied out several columns of the first Isaiah scroll before he returned the scrolls to the Metropolitan on 6 February 1948. Later he published what he had copied without the knowledge and consent of the Metropolitan.

In the same February, the Metropolitan contacted the American School of Oriental Research in Jerusalem (as it was then named; later it became the W. F. Albright Institute of Archaeological Research). Eventually, the Metropolitan sent the scrolls there. A Fellow of the School, John C. Trever, during the absence of its director, obtained permission from the Metropolitan to photograph three of the scrolls; the fourth was too difficult to unroll. Trever subsequently sent photographs of some of the scrolls to Prof. William F. Albright, of the Johns Hopkins University in Baltimore, Maryland, who confirmed Trever's judgment about the antiquity and value of the scrolls and wrote to Trever about them. Millar Burrows, a professor from Yale University and director of the American School, had been absent (in Iraq) when all of this took place. On his return, he too confirmed the authenticity and antiquity of the scrolls. The Metropolitan then sent the valuable scrolls to a place of safekeeping outside of Palestine, because of the developing unsafe political situation there. After the British Mandate came to an end (14 May 1948) and the State of Israel came into existence, Sukenik published some of his scrolls in *Megillot Genuzot I* in September 1948.

In January 1949, a Belgian soldier, Capt. Philippe Lippens, who was an observer for the United Nations in the area, made his way with a captain of the Jordanian Arab Legion to Qumran, and they soon found where the cave was located. Lippens alerted the Jordanian antiquities authority about the location of the cave. Père Roland de Vaux, O.P., director and archaeologist of the École Biblique et Archéologique Française in Jerusalem, along with G. Lankester Harding, the head of the Department of Antiquities in Jordan, investigated the cave, and then excavated it from 15 February to 5 March 1949. They found further fragments of the scrolls and other artifacts, thus confirming that the scrolls had indeed come from that cave. Subsequently, de Vaux and Lankester Harding, realizing that Cave 1 was not far from Khirbet Qumran, wondered whether the two might be related. They decided to excavate that site as well. De Vaux began the excavation of Khirbet Qumran on 24 November and continued until 12 December 1951. When he found pottery of the same kind as that from Cave 1 and a jar of the same sort, he realized that Cave 1 and Khirbet Qumran were related indeed. The excavations at Khirbet Qumran continued for four annual seasons thereafter.

In the meantime, the Metropolitan Athanasius Yeshue Samuel traveled to the United States in January of 1949, taking with him the four scrolls that he had acquired. While there, he negotiated with the American School of Oriental Research, based in New Haven, Connecticut, for the publication of the photographs and transcribed texts of those scrolls. The scrolls were put on exhibition in museums in Washington, DC; Baltimore, Maryland; Worcester, Massachusetts; and at Duke University in Durham, North Carolina. In January of 1950, volume 1 of *The Dead Sea Scrolls of St Mark's Monastery* was published.[1] It contained the Isaiah Manuscript (1QIsa^a) and the Commentary of Habakkuk (1QpHab). In February of 1951, the second fascicle of volume 2 was published, containing the Manual of Discipline (or Rule Book of the Community, 1QS).[2] The first fascicle of volume 2 was reserved for the Aramaic Genesis Apocryphon (1QapGen), which had proved difficult to unroll because it was so poorly preserved.

While the Metropolitan was engaged in all these transactions in the United States, the Ta'âmireh Bedouin of the West Bank, who had realized that they could profit financially from other written material and artifacts, began looking for other possible caves that might contain such material. They discovered in October of 1951 some documents in caves of the Wadi Murabbaʿat, which lies about 12 miles southwest of Qumran, and which de Vaux and Lankester Harding later excavated (21 January to 3 March 1952). These caves yielded interesting documents: from the time of the Second Jewish Revolt against Roman domination (A.D. 132–135), letters of Simon ben Kosiba (Bar Kokhba), and so forth. In February of 1952, the Bedouin found Qumran Cave 2, not far removed from Cave 1, from which they removed all the fragments. There were 33 small texts, nothing so important as those of the first cave.

These discoveries moved the archaeologists to conduct a thorough investigation of the cliffs of the whole region from 10 to 29 March 1952. During this time, they surveyed roughly eight kilometers of the cliffs north and south of Khirbet Qumran, from Hajar al-ʿAṣbaʾ (or in Hebrew, ʾEben habbohen [Josh 15:6]) to Ras Feshkha. They explored about 50 caves and holes, in 25 of which they found artifacts and pottery of the same sort as in Cave 1 and Khirbet Qumran. More importantly, though, they discovered Qumran Cave 3 on 20 March, with its so-called Copper Scroll and 14 fragmentary texts—a discovery made by archaeologists, and not by Bedouin! The latter were still searching, and in July of 1952 they came upon nearly a hundred writings in different languages (Arabic, Greek, Christian Palestinian Syriac) at Khirbet Mird (Castellion, Marda). This site was not near the Wadis Qumran or Murabbaʿat, but above the cliffs and in the desert, about 15 km southeast of Jerusalem. The site was explored eventually (February to April 1953) by the Belgian Capt. P. Lippens and R. de Langhe, a professor at the University of Louvain in Belgium.

While de Vaux was excavating the plateau at Khirbet Qumran in 1952, the Bedouin opened up another cave a few hundred feet away from the buildings being uncovered at Khirbet Qumran. This was Qumran Cave 4, and it turned out to be the most important of all the caves, not only of those already found but also those yet to be found. It yielded about 582 fragmentary documents, but not one of them was whole or complete. It is often called "the Cave of the Partridge," because one of the elderly men of the tribe remembered that, when he was young, he was hunting and saw a partridge fly into a hole on top of the plateau. So younger Bedouin tribesmen went looking for the hole in 1952, found it, and opened it up to discover a two-room cave that had been artificially hollowed out in the marly surface of the south edge of the plateau, which overlooked the Wadi Qumran itself. About 15,000 fragments were retrieved, many of them by the Bedouin, from whom authorities of the Jordanian government in Jerusalem and various foreign institutions eventually bought them, at a sum of 15,000 Jordanian dinars (about $42,000). The archaeologists de Vaux and Lankester Harding, along with J. T. Milik, soon learned about the discovery, put an end to the Bedouin activity there, and then cleaned out the rest of the cave (22 to 29 September 1952).

In the meantime, while de Vaux and others were working on Cave 4, Milik and other archaeologists came upon another cave nearby, which Milik himself excavated (25–29 September) and from which he retrieved 25 fragmentary texts, biblical and nonbiblical, and many artifacts and pottery types. This was Qumran Cave 5. About the same time, the Bedouin uncovered still another cave nearby, Qumran Cave 6, which yielded 31 fragmentary documents.

In 1954, the three scrolls from Cave 1 (1QIsa^b, 1QH^a, 1QM) that Sukenik had acquired were finally published posthumously.[3]

The excavations at Khirbet Qumran continued in the following years, as already indicated above. During the fourth season of excavation (1955), the archaeologists discovered the remains of Caves 7–10 at the southern end of the plateau, also overlooking the Wadi Qumran. These caves had eroded and tumbled into the Wadi below in the course of the centuries, but enough of them remained from which fragmentary texts were retrieved: from Cave 7, 19 texts (all in Greek!); from Cave 8, five texts; from Caves 9 and 10, one text each.

In January 1956, the Bedouin discovered in the cliffs well north of Khirbet Qumran—ironically enough, in the very cliffs that the archaeologists had explored in early 1952—yet another cave, which yielded 31 texts, some of them nearly complete. This was Qumran Cave 11. The news of its discovery made the archaeologists undertake another expedition there from 18 February to 28 March 1956.

Finally, de Vaux and his team of archaeologists turned their attention to 'Ain Feshkha, a site about a mile and a half south of Khirbet Qumran, where there was a spring gushing with slightly brackish water, to which the Bedouins often led their flocks. There the excavations, carried out from 25 January to 21 March 1958, uncovered the remains of a storage barn, several pools, a shed where dates were hung to be dried, and an enclosure in which flocks were kept.

In March and April 1960, an exploration was undertaken to the valleys between En Gedi and Masada. At Naḥal Ṣe'elim, biblical fragments and Hebrew and Greek papyrus texts were discovered in what came to be called the "Cave of the Scrolls." In Naḥal Ḥever, fifteen letters of Simon ben Kosiba (Bar Kokhba) were uncovered in the "Cave of Letters." In the following year in the same valley, Aramaic, Hebrew, and Nabatean deeds were retrieved from the "Cave of Horror," and the Archive of Babatha in the "Cave of Letters."

In 1963–1965, archaeologists explored Masada itself, where they found fragments of OT texts, a fragmentary copy of Ben Sira, and fragments of the *Book of Jubilees*, and the so-called Angelic Liturgy.

Because so many texts had been retrieved from Qumran caves 2–10, especially from Cave 4, a decision was made to set up an international and interconfessional team of scholars who would work on them. The fragmentary texts had been brought to what was then called the Palestine Archaeological Museum in east Jerusalem (since 1967 renamed the Rockefeller Museum). The scholars were chosen from different European and American universities but related to various archaeological institutions in Jordanian-controlled Jerusalem, for example, the École Biblique, the American School of Oriental Research (now known as the W. F. Albright Institute of Archaeological Research), and British and German archaeological institutions based in Jerusalem. Two were Americans: Frank M. Cross, a Presbyterian, then professor at the McCormick Theological Seminary in Chicago (later at Harvard University), and Patrick W. Skehan, a Catholic, professor at the Catholic University of America in Washington, DC; two were British: John Strugnell, a Presbyterian (later a convert to Catholicism), a recent graduate of Jesus College, University of Oxford, and John M. Allegro, an agnostic, lecturer at the University of Manchester; one was French: Jean Starcky, a Catholic priest, attached to the Centre National de la Recherche Scientifique; one was Polish: Jozef T. Milik, a Catholic priest (a recent student at the Biblical Institute in Rome); and one was German: Claus-Hunno Hunzinger, a Lutheran, from the University of Göttingen; after a short time, he retired from the team, and his place was taken by a Frenchman, Maurice Baillet, a Catholic priest, from Toulouse. Père Roland de Vaux was appointed director of the team by G. Lankester Harding, the head of the Department of Antiquities in Jordan. The team was appointed to work on all the fragments of Caves 2–10, but mainly on the 15,000 fragments from Cave 4, which constituted a giant jigsaw puzzle that had to be pieced together. In addition, there were the 72 fragments of Cave 1 that the archaeologists had retrieved in their excavation, and also the texts from Cave 11, which would be discovered in 1956.

Despite the fact that competent Israeli scholars lived nearby, even in west Jerusalem, none of them became members of that team. The reason for this exclusion was the political situation of Jerusalem at that time. Although Cave 1 had been discovered in 1947 in territory then controlled by the British Mandate of Palestine, the rest of the Qumran caves were found in the West Bank, then under Jordanian control, as was east Jerusalem, where the Palestine Archaeological Museum was found and where the scrolls and fragments were being worked on. East and west Jerusalem were divided from each other by a high stone wall and a mined no-man's-land. So no Jewish scholar was able to cross over into east Jerusalem and become part of the team. It was not owing to any prejudice against Jewish scholars, as has been said at times, but simply to the political situation of the city of Jerusalem.

The story of the discovery of the scrolls moved in a different direction in 1954. The four scrolls that the Metropolitan, Mar Athanasius Yeshue Samuel, had brought to the United States remained in his possession, although he had tried to sell them. He did not succeed at first, because no one wanted to put up a considerable amount of money for documents, valuable though they were, the ownership of which was still in doubt. Then, however, an advertisement appeared in the Wall Street Journal of 1 June 1954: "'THE FOUR DEAD SEA SCROLLS' Biblical Manuscripts dating back to at least 200 B.C. are for sale. This would be an ideal gift to an educational or religious institution by an individual or group. Box F

SCROLLS CAVE SIGN FROM PRESENT-DAY QUMRAN SITE

206." The advertisement came to the attention of Yigael Yadin, the son of Prof. Sukenik who had acquired the three other manuscripts of Cave 1. Yadin, a former officer in the Israeli Army during the first Arab–Jewish War and subsequently Deputy Prime Minister of Israel, was in the United States at that time, and he arranged to purchase, on 1 July of that year, the four manuscripts through a New York banker as middleman for $250,000. The next day the scrolls were taken to the Israeli Consulate in New York and eventually were sent, one by one, to Jerusalem. Yadin presented them to the State of Israel, where they joined the other three. All seven scrolls are housed today in the Shrine of the Book, part of the Israel Museum in Jerusalem. The fourth scroll was subsequently unrolled and named the "Genesis Apocryphon." The best part of it was published by Israeli scholars in 1956,[4] and another part of it in 1992. The official publication of this scroll in its entirety is still awaited.

The result of this remarkable find between 1947 and 1956 has been hailed as "the greatest manuscript discovery of modern times" (W. F. Albright). It is a tribute to the Bedouin Arabs, who accomplished most of it. Who knows how many more hidden caves still conceal ancient written documents that will make the impact on the study of Palestinian Judaism and its biblical books that these eleven Qumran caves have made! These Qumran Scrolls have supplied texts that fall into three groups: (1) biblical texts (copies of every book of the OT, except Esther); (2) sectarian texts (rulebooks, liturgical, and poetic writings); and (3) parabiblical Jewish documents, often misnamed "intertestamental" (*Enoch, Jubilees,* etc.).

This discovery of scrolls and fragments in Qumran Caves 1–11 in the years 1947–1956 was not the first such discovery. Long ago, in the third century, Origen (185–254) composed the *Hexapla,* a six-column text with the OT in Hebrew and in differing Greek versions. He reported that he used for the sixth column Greek texts that had been found together with other Hebrew and Greek writings in a jar near Jericho. Later, the church historian Eusebius (260–340) also recorded that Origen has used a text "found at Jericho in a jar in the time of Antoninus, son of Severus" (*Eccles. Hist.* 6.16.1). Still later, Timotheos I, the Nestorian Patriarch (727–819), wrote that "some books were found in a cave near Jericho," which contemporary Jews identified as "the OT and other writings in Hebrew."

Such testimonies show that the Qumran discoveries were not the first. At the end of the nineteenth century, in 1896, Solomon Schechter found in the genizah of the Synagogue of Fustat (Old Cairo) a text that he published under the title *Fragments of a Zadokite Work,* not knowing what it really was. It turned out to be a medieval copy of a rule book similar to the Manual of Discipline (1QS), and is known today as the Damascus Document. Further copies of it were retrieved from Qumran Cave 4 (eight copies, 4Q266–273), and one copy each from Cave 5 (5Q12) and Cave 6 (6Q15).

Dating

The major problem that the scrolls and fragments from the eleven Qumran caves create is the determination of their antiquity: How old are they? Many have been those who doubted that they were really ancient. For instance, as early as August 1947, a Dutch Dominican, J. P. M. van der Ploeg, O.P., while visiting the École

Biblique in Jerusalem, was shown the manuscript of the Isaiah from Qumran Cave 1 (1QIsa^a). He recognized it as a copy of Isaiah but failed to see it as ancient. Later, when texts of Cave 1 were published in the United States, an American Jewish scholar, Solomon Zeitlin of Dropsie College in Philadelphia, labeled them all a medieval "hoax."[5] About the same time, a Jewish scholar in Great Britain, J. L. Teicher, maintained that the Qumran Scrolls emanated from the Jewish Christian sect of the Ebionites.[6] He thus assigned the scrolls a date in the second or third Christian century. Some time later, Cecil Roth, also of Great Britain, attributed the scrolls to the Zealots, the radical and xenophobic rebels who were active in Palestine about the time of the First Jewish Revolt against Roman rule (A.D. 66–70).[7]

Such an attribution confined the Jewish Qumran Scrolls again to the Christian period. These diverse opinions reveal the problem of the dating of the scrolls.

The Qumran Scrolls are unlike many of the documents that bear an ancient date, for example, texts from the Murabba'at caves, or from Wadi Seiyal, because none of them bears a date. There are, however, references or allusions in some of them to historical persons: for example, "Demetrius, king of Greece" (= Demetrios III Eukairos) or cryptic references to historical events: for example, Kittim (the code-name for the Roman occupiers of Palestine). Some of the references are clear and can be confirmed by evidence in the writings of Josephus, the Jewish historian, but others are difficult to interpret correctly. One has to realize also that the date that can be ascertained for a given text is only the date of the copy; it says nothing about the date of the composition of the work that it contains.

Most of the scholars who have studied the QL date it roughly from 200–150 B.C. to A.D. 68. The reason for such a dating is determined mainly by three factors:

(1) *Archaeological Data.* As I shall show in chapter II, the data gathered from the excavation of the caves and the ruins of Khirbet Qumran favor a comprehensive period that begins before the Roman period of ancient Palestine and continues in the first Christian century up to a short time before the destruction of Jerusalem in A.D. 70. Such evidence comes from the pottery, coins, and other artifacts found there, as well as from radiocarbon dating of some arti-

facts. There is also the evidence of a rift caused by an earthquake, which according to Josephus, the Jewish historian, hit the area in the year 31 B.C. (*Ant.* 15.5.1 §§121–22). The scrolls would date to this period ascertained by archaeological means.

(2) *Palaeographical Data.* Palaeography is the study of the way scribes shaped the Hebrew and Aramaic letters on documents and texts. Since styles change and develop with the passage of time, a palaeographer can locate where a particular document belongs in the development. In antiquity, documents were written usually by trained or professional scribes, and this also aids palaeographers in their analysis. There are, moreover, sufficient ancient Hebrew and Aramaic texts from various localities that display the differences; some of them from places other than Qumran even bear dates, such as papyri from Elephantine in Egypt, or from Masada, which fell to the Romans in A.D. 73–74. Such dates enable the palaeographer to situate a text in a line of scribal development. The palaeography of the Qumran texts was worked out, as early as 1961, by F. M. Cross, now professor emeritus of Harvard University, along with help from the Polish scholar J. T. Milik. They showed that the script, which was used for both Aramaic and Hebrew, should be divided into four groups: (a) Archaic script, dating roughly from 250 to 150 B.C.; (b) Hasmonean script, from 150 to 30 B.C.; (c) Herodian script, from 30 B.C. to A.D. 68; (d) Post-Herodian script, from A.D. 68 on.[8] Cross further subdivided the groups as formal, semiformal, cursive, and semicursive—the latter two being found often in texts not written by trained scribes. The vast majority of the Qumran documents belong to either the Hasmonean or the Herodian group. This palaeographic analysis at times has been controversial, and for that reason scholars have looked often for other methods of dating.

(3) *Radiocarbon Analysis of the Scrolls.* Carbon-14 is a radioactive isotope that breaks down at a precisely measurable rate independently of its environment. Cosmic rays from outer space, bombarding the earth with apparent constancy, change nitrogen in the earth's atmosphere into Carbon-14. When Carbon-14 reacts with oxygen in the air, it produces carbon dioxide. Plants derive most of their carbon from carbon dioxide in air and water; animals feed on plants, and so all living things end up with some radioactive Carbon-14. When an organism dies, it dies with a certain amount of carbon

and Carbon-14. The latter continues to radiate, but it does not take in further carbon; it also begins to break down and turn back into nitrogen. This breakdown continues at a constant rate, and its "half-life" is measurable: the time during which one half of its contained radiant energy decays. Measuring organic material by the rate of time it takes for this breakdown yields a date that enables scientists to tell when the material existed.

This method of analysis, first discovered in 1947, was not used on any of the skin or papyrus on which the documents had been written. It was applied, however, in 1951 to some of the linen in which the scrolls of Qumran Cave 1 had been wrapped. The date the linen yielded was A.D. 33 ± 200 years, which would mean 168 B.C.–A.D. 233. Later it was applied to palm wood from Khirbet Qumran, which yielded a date of 7 B.C.–A.D. 18. Although this method proved valuable, it was not used on the skin or papyrus of the Qumran texts, because it required the loss of some of it.

More recently, the radiocarbon analysis has been refined. A process has been developed called "accelerator mass spectronomy" (AMS), for which only a miniscule amount of the material is lost. This method was then applied to the skins of Qumran texts in 1990. Eight Qumran texts and six documents from other sites were used, among them four with dates (which were not mentioned to the scientists who did the testing—so that the process might not be compromised from the outset). The first testing was done at the Institut für Mittelenergiephysik in Zurich, Switzerland. In the case of the Qumran documents, seven of the eight, which had been dated palaeographically, fell within the dates obtained by AMS; for the eighth document (4Q534 [now known as 4Q542], 4QTKohath), the date obtained by AMS (388–353 B.C.) was much earlier than the palaeographic date (100–75 B.C.).[9] Why this difference occurred is not known; possibly the skin was contaminated in some way.

Using such methods, scholars studying the Qumran texts have been able to assign dates to them. For instance, the complete Isaiah scroll from Cave 1 (lQIs[a]) is dated 125–100 B.C.; 4QSam[c] is dated 100–75 B.C.

II

THE DEAD SEA SCROLLS:
Archaeology, the Excavation of Khirbet Qumran

The Dead Sea lies 1,264 feet below sea level at the base of the Great Rift Valley. In Hebrew it is called *Yam hammelaḥ,* "Sea of Salt," and in Latin it is known as *Lacus Asphaltites,* "The Asphalt Lake." Sitting back from its northwest shore about half a mile is a row of high cliffs, beyond which is part of the Judean Desert. The cliffs stretch about five miles from Hajar al-'Aṣba' in the north to Ras Feshkha in the south, a promontory that juts into the Dead Sea. Roughly in the middle of the five miles, there is the Wadi Qumran, a torrent-bed through which water flows in the rainy season from the desert and cliffs westward into the Dead Sea. Immediately to the north of the wadi is a plateau about 75 feet high close to the cliffs. On the plateau one finds the ancient ruins of Khirbet Qumran and to the east of them a large cemetery, separated from the ruins by a long wall.

Archaeology

After the connection between Qumran Cave 1 and Khirbet Qumran had been established, Roland de Vaux undertook the excavation of the ancient ruins on the latter site. He worked at the site for five years: 24 November to 12 December, 1951; 9 February to 24 April 1953; 15 February to 15 April 1954; 2 February to 6 April 1955; and 18 February to 28 March 1956.

15

Khirbet Qumran

The stone ruins of Qumran had been dated often to Roman times, and some investigators of the site thought they were the remains of a Roman fort, whereas others considered them the remains of a small town (perhaps Gomorrah [Gen 19:24], or City of Salt [Josh 15:62]). When de Vaux and Lankester Harding in 1951 made a sounding at the ruins, they discovered pottery, which related the ruins to those of Cave 1, and so they were sure that the site had to be excavated.

De Vaux undertook the first session of excavation in November–December of that year, and continued the excavation for four more years. He wrote preliminary reports of his excavations every year in the *Revue Biblique*, and later he summarized these reports in the Schweich Lectures that he was asked to deliver before the British Academy in 1959; they were published subsequently as a book, *L'Archéologie et les manuscrits de la Mer Morte*.[1] De Vaux identified three principal periods of occupation at Khirbet Qumran:

(1) An Iron Age village of the eighth–seventh century B.C., at the lowest level of the site. This was perhaps the City of Salt, mentioned above. The pottery retrieved gave evidence of the Iron Age. Remains of a rectangular building also were uncovered, possibly one of the many "towers in the wilderness" constructed by King Uzziah (2 Chr 26:9–10). Likewise belonging to this period was the round cistern (§110 on the plan of the site).

(2) The site of the sect of Palestinian Jews who used the scrolls found in the Qumran caves. This is a rectangular area about 80 x 90 meters, with the remains of what must have been a lofty tower in the northwest corner. The entrance to the complex was through a doorway in a wall running to the north from the corner of the tower. As one enters, one notices the remains of a lengthy aqueduct that brought water from the cliffs and the Wadi Qumran to various areas in the main building. Between the periods 1 and 2, a lapse of several centuries ensued, and period 2 spanned the better part of two centuries, roughly from 130 B.C. to A.D. 68. De Vaux divided this period into two parts:

PRESENT-DAY QUMRAN ARCHAEOLOGICAL SITE

(a) *Phase Ia*. In this phase, some remains of the old Israelite construction were reused, for example, the round cistern; but other rooms were built anew, and kilns were erected for the making of pottery.

(b) *Phase Ib*. This phase was the far more important period. It was begun during the reign of the Hasmonean king and high priest John Hyrcanus (134–104 B.C.). It lasted until 31 B.C., when the structures were burnt, apparently as a result of the earthquake that hit the area in the seventh year of the reign of Herod the Great (Josephus, *Ant.* 15.5.2 §121). In this phase, the Jewish sect built an aqueduct of 750 meters to bring water in the rainy seasons from the Wadi Qumran to seven rectangular cisterns (§§49, 56, 71, 117, 118) and baths in the buildings. They also constructed a defense tower (§8–10) on the foundations that dated from the Iron Age period, and a main building of at least two stories, with a staircase (§13), a dining room (§77), a pantry (§86), a council chamber (§4), a scriptorium (writing room §30) on the second story. (The remains of a table and two inkwells were found above the remains of a floor that had crashed to the ground below.) In a clearly marked industrial quarter (§§103–123) and elsewhere in the complex, the sectarians had constructed a barn, kilns for firing pottery, ovens, a dyer's shop, a laundry, and so on. No manuscripts or fragments were found in this center, but jars, inscribed ostraca, and many coins were retrieved; several jars contained animal bones, but the purpose of such jars is unknown.

There is no evidence, however, of any living quarters, and so de Vaux concluded that the whole place served not as a residence but as a community center, to which the sectarians came for various common events (meals, meetings, prayers, etc.). He also concluded that the sectarians lived round about in huts and caves in the cliffs, where evidence of human occupation was found, artifacts and pottery that resembled the sort found in Khirbet Qumran. De Vaux maintained that the site was abandoned after the fire and earthquake and that a time-gap ensued before the site was rebuilt.

(c) *Phase II.* This phase, according to de Vaux, was begun in 4 B.C., after the death of Herod the Great, when the site was reconstructed in almost the same shape and size as it had been in phase Ib. The base of the defense tower (§8–10) was fortified with a curved revetment about four meters high. Only a few coins of Herod the Great were found, but a good number of Archelaus, his successor on the throne. This phase lasted until A.D. 68, when the buildings were burnt again. This time they were destroyed by the Roman legions (Legio X Fretensis and Legio XV Apollinaris) that had descended the valley of the Jordan River and were en route to besiege Jerusalem, which they captured in A.D. 70. Eighty-three bronze coins of the second year of the Revolt against Rome reveal that the site was razed by the Romans, and distinctive Roman three-winged arrowheads were found in the ashes of the destroying fire.

(3) *Phase III.* This period was that of Roman occupation; it lasted until about A.D. 90. Roman soldiers built some crude barracks on the remains of the sectarian site, mainly in the southwestern corner of the main building.

'Ain Feshkha

In 1958, de Vaux also excavated the site of 'Ain Feshkha, which was recognized to be related to Khirbet Qumran only in 1956. There is a spring at 'Ain Feshkha, with brackish water, and to the north of it the sectarians constructed a large building, flanked on the south side by a large enclosure with sheds for animals, and by a courtyard with basins on the north side. The building itself measures 24 x 18 meters, and though some rooms were used for habitation, most of them were for storage. In the area immediately to the west of the main construction was a hangar for the drying of dates. The basins had been filled with water, perhaps for fish, but also for treating of skins to be used in scrolls. The building and its surroundings were constructed at the end of Phase Ib and used mostly in Phase II. Later on, the whole area was used during Phase III; still later, Christian monks in the Byzantine period occupied part of it.

Cemetery

To the east of the community center on the plateau was a large cemetery, separated from the buildings by a long wall, which stopped about four meters from the western edge of the cemetery. Thus the living were freed from any contact with the dead, which would have been ritually defiling.

About 1,100 tombs have been counted; these are marked by rectangular piles of stones, with the short sides running east and west and the long sides running north and south. The tombs are oriented, then, north–south. The tombs are arranged in rows with a small aisle between them. During the excavation of the buildings of the community center, de Vaux opened about 26 of the tombs in different areas of the cemetery. The skeletons were enclosed in boxes and deposited about a meter and a half below the surface, in a loculus dug into the east wall of the tomb and protected from the earth above by flat stones or bricks. The head of the skeleton lay to the south, so that the buried person was looking toward the north. In the vast majority of the tombs that were opened, the skeleton was that of a male; in only one was a female skeleton found. De Vaux also investigated two smaller cemeteries nearby, in which male and female skeletons had been buried; and in one tomb the skeletons of a woman and three children were found.

SHRINE OF THE BOOK AT THE ISRAEL MUSEUM, JERUSALEM, WHERE
MANY OF THE DEAD SEA SCROLLS ARE LOCATED

The cemetery had been noticed by many scholars who had vis-ited the remains, and some tombs had been opened up.[2] Its nature, however, puzzled almost all of them because of the north–south alignment of the tombs. In the Near Eastern area of that period, tombs of Jews and Arabs were aligned usually east–west. Moreover, there was no reason to think that Christians had been buried there. No one had been able to date the burials, because what tombs had been opened contained only skeletons and no accompanying burial objects. Now, however, with the discovery of the caves with written material and the excavation of Khirbet Qumran, it became apparent that the tombs contained the remains of a community of Jews who dwelt in the Qumran area and used the community center.

Controversy

The reconstruction and interpretation of the archaeological evidence given by de Vaux have proved acceptable, in general, to many scholars who have studied the results of his work. Some scholars or archaeologists, however, have either rejected his entire interpretation or queried some details. For instance, the time-gap that de Vaux postulated between Phase Ia and Phase Ib has been questioned almost from the time that he proposed it. Moreover, the archaeological evidence for Phase Ia is so sparse that qualified archaeologists who have examined the remains wonder whether there were such a phase. Part of the difficulty is that de Vaux died in 1971, before he was able to publish the final report of his excavations, and his reasons for the interpretation of some details have remained unknown. In the last decade or so, the final report has been published.[3] Other archaeologists have published reports on excavations of Khirbet Qumran and 'Ain Feshkha, for example, a colleague of de Vaux, who worked with him at Khirbet Qumran, E.-M. Laperrousaz.[4] His report, by and large, agrees with de Vaux. Others, however, have disagreed. Whereas de Vaux interpreted Khirbet Qumran as a sectarian settlement, a community center around which Jews lived in caves and huts, the Belgians Robert and Pauline Donceel-Voûte regarded it as a luxurious Villa Rustica, and for them the scriptorium was a dining room.[5] Norman Golb, of the University of Chicago, rejected de Vaux's interpretation entirely and maintained that the site was rather a fort and that the scrolls had nothing to do with Khirbet Qumran, having been brought rather from Jerusalem.[6] Likewise disagreeing with de Vaux is Yizhar Hirschfeld, a professor of archaeology at the Hebrew University in Jerusalem, who interprets the evidence from Khirbet Qumran and 'Ain Feshkha in a wider historical-geographical background and concludes that, though there may have been some Essenes living on the fringes of the Qumran estate, the upper class who lived there had nothing to do with a community, and their remains are an amazing assemblage of rich objects.[7]

In contrast to such interpretations of the excavations at Qumran put forth by the Donceels, Golb, and Hirschfeld, stands that of Jodi Magness, who offers good correctives of de Vaux's interpretation but basically agrees with him.[8] She had access to many of the field notes and the pottery collection of de Vaux, even before they began to be published.

Magness maintains that there is no clear evidence for Phase Ia. There are no coins from that phase, and the pottery retrieved differs little from that of Phase Ib. What de Vaux called Phase Ia did not end with destruction. One has to subdivide rather what he called Phase Ib into two levels: Pre-31 (from 100/50 to 31 B.C.) and Post-31 (from 31 to 9/8 or 4 B.C.). Moreover, since the coins of Alexander Jannaeus (103–76 B.C.) found in this phase at Khirbet Qumran continued in circulation until Herod the Great, the beginning of the sectarian settlement must have been sometime in the first century B.C., and not toward the last third of the second century, as de Vaux had proposed. Likewise, it does not make sense that the site was unoccupied from 31 to 4 B.C. Phase II would have been from 4/1 B.C. to A.D. 68.

III

THE PALESTINIAN JEWISH SECT OF THE ESSENES:
History and Organization

Identification

The Jews who wrote or used the collection of documents known today as the Qumran Scrolls are not easy to identify. Their origin in pre-Christian times is certain, as the archaeological evidence from Khirbet Qumran, 'Ain Feshkha, and the caves in which the texts were found makes clear. Unfortunately, there is nothing in any of the documents that reveals who they were; the members of the sect do not reveal their name(s), except by indirect appellations, such as *yaḥad*, "community" (literally, "unit"), which occurs in the title of its rule book (DJD 1. 107; pl. XXII); *běnê Ṣādôq*, "sons of Zadoq" (1QS 5:2, 9); *'anšê hayyaḥad*, "men of the community" (1QS 5:1); *běnê 'ôr*, "sons of light" (1QS 1:9; 1QM 1:1); *běrît haḥădāšāh*, "the new covenant" (1QpHab 2:3; CD 6:19 [name derived from Jer 31:31]); *bā'ê habběrît*, "those who enter the covenant" (1QS 2:18); *'ēdāh*, "congregation" (1QSa 1:6); *'ădat hā-'ebyônîm*, "congregation of the poor" (4QpPs[a] [4Q171] 2:10); *šābê Yiśrā'ēl*, "the returnees of Israel" (CD 4:2); *ḥibbûr Yiśrā'ēl*, "the company of Israel" (CD 12:8); or *qāhāl*, "assembly" (1QSa 1:25). None of these symbolic titles, however, tells us anything about their historical name.

Consequently, many attempts have been made by modern scholars to identify the inhabitants, using names derived from other historical documents that have revealed the different kinds of Jews who lived in ancient Palestine or Judea. For instance, the Sadducees (G. Margoliouth, R. North, L. H. Schiffman); Pharisees (C. Rabin);

Herodians (C. Daniel); Qaraites (S. Zeitlin, P. R. Weiss). The most commonly proposed identification, however, is the Essenes; this was proposed first by E. L. Sukenik and, independently, by the French scholar A. Dupont-Sommer. Some scholars, however, have even maintained that the people of the scrolls were Christians (R. H. Eisenman, B. Thiering), and specifically Ebionites (O. Cullmann, J. L. Teicher).

Essenes

The historical name "Essene" is passed on in various spellings in Greek and Latin sources. One finds the Greek spelling *Essēnoi* in some manuscripts of Josephus's writings, and *Essaioi* in others. Writers of the patristic period (e.g., Epiphanius) sometimes have the Greek spelling *Ossēnoi* or *Ossaioi* (a copyist's confusion of ε with O?). In Latin, the name is given as *Esseni* (so Pliny the Elder [*Nat. Hist.* 5.15.73]). Even though this name is used for Jews, no one has ever found such a name in Hebrew or Aramaic texts. Some scholars have tried to explain *Essēnoi* as an adjective (with the common Greek gentilic ending *-ēnos*) derived either from the Hebrew root *'sy*, "do, make" (hence "Doers" [i.e., those that do the will of God]), or "heal" (hence "Healers"), or *ḥasayyā'*, "pious ones" (Aramaic). None of these explanations is really convincing.

The reason why most scholars prefer to identify the Qumran sect as Essene is the testimony of the Latin writer Pliny the Elder (Gaius Plinius Secundus, A.D. 23–79). In his *Naturalis historia* he described the land of Judea, and having mentioned the town of Jericho, he moved to the Dead Sea. Part of his description of this area runs as follows (5.15.73):

> To the west [of the Dead Sea], the Essenes [*Esseni*] have withdrawn from the insalubrious shore [of the sea]. They are a unique group of people, admirable beyond all others in the whole world: [they live] without women, without sexual intercourse, without money—with date palms for their only companions! Day by day, owing to the arrival of newcomers, this people steadily is reborn, as

SIGN FROM QUMRAN EXHIBIT SITE

large numbers stream there who are weary of life and driven by waves of fortune to [adopt] their manners. So for thousands of ages, incredible to recount, a people lives on among whom no one is born; so fruitful for them is the penitence of others for their past lives.

Below them was [formerly] the town of Engada [modern 'En Gedi], second only to Jerusalem in fertility and groves of palm trees, but now another heap of ashes. From there [one comes to] Masada, a fortress [situated] on a crag, not too far distant from the Dead Sea. Up to this point is the boundary of Judea.

Pliny was a Roman writer who died in A.D. 79 from fumes caused by the eruption of Mount Vesuvius. He was aware of the destruction of Jerusalem, as the second paragraph of the quotation implies. He wrote some remarkable things about the Essenes, whom he scarcely understood correctly: for example, his assertion that the Essenes existed "for thousands of ages." Many other of the details he provides, however, have proven to be correct, when his descrip-

25

tion is compared with the account of the Essenes given by Josephus, Philo of Alexandria, and now with details from the Qumran Scrolls. Moreover, his description fits well with the location of Khirbet Qumran, because it is the only sizable site south of Jericho and north of 'En Gedi and Masada that matches it.

The Jewish historian Flavius Josephus (A.D. 37–100?) wrote (about A.D. 66) his *Jewish War*, a description of the conflict that the Jews of Judea had with the Romans, which resulted in the destruction of Jerusalem and its Temple. In it he described what he called the three "philosophies" of the Jews: the sects of the Pharisees, of the Sadducees, and of the Essenes (*J.W.* 2.8.14 §§119–66).[1] His description of the Essenes is longer than that of either the Pharisees or the Sadducees, showing how highly Josephus regarded them, despite the fact that biblical accounts present the latter two sects as far more important. The passage in *J.W.* to which I have just referred is too long to be quoted here; so the reader should consult a reliable translation of it.[2]

Here is a brief summary of the main details that Josephus recounts about the Essenes: They are one of the three main sects among the Jews of his day, a close-knit people "like brothers" (§122); many of them do not marry, but a few do (§§119, 160); they live in community, despise wealth, and hold all things in common (§122); they consider oil a defilement and dress in white garments (§123); they dwell in many towns throughout Judea (§124 [but no mention of a desert retreat or of Qumran!]); they pray with prayers handed on by their ancestors (§128); they work industriously at crafts assigned to them by superiors (§129); they take their meals in common, eating what is put before them, after a priest has given thanks (§§130–31); they do nothing without orders from superiors (§134); they hold their tempers in check and swear no oaths (§135); they read the writings of ancients (§136); they have strict procedures for accepting candidates to their sect (§137); those who have been found guilty of serious crimes are expelled (§143); they strictly observe the Law of Moses (§145); they are stricter than all other Jews in observing the Sabbath (§147); they have strict regulations for use of the toilet (§§148–49); they are divided into four grades or ranks (§150); they live long lives and believe that they will enjoy an afterlife (§§154–58); they believe in predestination (*Ant.* 13.5.9

§172 [called "fate" here]); they send offerings to the Jerusalem Temple, but offer their own sacrifices according to a different ritual (*Ant.*18.1.5 §19 [which is not indicated]). Josephus gives the number of Essenes as "four thousand" (*Ant.* 18.1.5 §20), but that number undoubtedly means the whole Essene movement in Judea, whereas the Essenes at Qumran must have numbered about 300 or 350 at most.

A similar, but less detailed, description of Essene life is provided by Philo of Alexandria (30 B.C.–A.D. 45), in his writings *Every Good Man Is Free* 12–13 §§75–91 and *Hypothetica* (*Apologia pro Iudaeis* 11.1–18). Philo also numbers the Essenes at "four thousand" (*Every Good Man...* §75). Philo also has another writing, *The Contemplative Life* 2 §§10–11, in which he describes a group of Jewish contemplatives, whom he calls "Therapeutae," who lived in solitude in various places in Egypt: celibate men and women, whom he relates to the Essenes of Judea.[3]

A brief notice of the Essenes is found also in Hippolytus of Rome, *Refutation of All Heresies* 9.18–28.[4] So much for the identification of the people behind the Qumran Scrolls and the site of Khirbet Qumran, according to the majority opinion today.

Origin of the Essenes

Two main explanations are current about the origin of the Jewish sect of the Essenes: one traces them to a Palestinian or Judean setting, and the other to a Babylonian background.

(1) *Palestinian or Judean Context.* In the early second century B.C., the Seleucid king of Syria, Antiochus IV Epiphanes (reigned 175–163 B.C.), sought to unify his kingdom by imposing Hellenistic culture on all the people, including the Jews of Judea; he thus tried to do away with Judaism (1 Macc 1:13–15). In December of 167 B.C., he defiled the Jerusalem Temple by sacrificing swine to Olympian Zeus on a Greek altar that he had had constructed there. This became known as "the abomination of desolation" (Dan 11:31). He also committed other atrocities throughout Judea (1 Macc 1:54–61). All of this led to the revolt of Jews under Mattathias, the great-grandson of Hashmon, an aged priest in Modein. Mattathias

refused to offer sacrifice to heathen Greek gods and killed an apostate Jew who was about to do so. This sparked what came to be known as the Maccabean Revolt (1 Macc 2:1–5). Among the five sons of Mattathias was one named Judas Maccabeus ("the hammer"), who eventually led the rebellion and became the ruler of Jerusalem and Judah (166–160 B.C.). Mattathias and his family fled from Jerusalem to the northwest part of Judah, and he invited all who were "zealous for the Law and supporters of the Covenant" (1 Macc 2:27–28) to come along. Thus emerged in Palestinian Judaism the company of Jews called *Ḥăsîdîm*, "Hasideans, mighty warriors of Israel, every one who offered himself willingly for the Law" (1 Macc 2:42; 7:13). Through their guerrilla-style warfare, they eventually took Jerusalem, purified it of the abomination of desolation, and rededicated it to the cult of the God of their ancestors. The rededication was remembered annually thereafter as *Ḥannûkāh* (John 10:22).

From the Maccabean Revolt emerged the Hasmonean dynasty, named after Hashmon (mentioned above). When Judas Maccabeus died in 160 B.C., he was succeeded by the youngest son of Mattathias, Jonathan, who ruled from 160 to 142 B.C. and was recognized as high priest by the Seleucid ruler, Alexander Balas, but he was not acknowledged to be such by most of the Jewish people. He was eventually assassinated by a Syrian soldier. Then the second son of Mattathias, Simon, succeeded Jonathan (142–134 B.C.), and he won independence for the Jews in Judea, having made a treaty with the Seleucid king Demetrius II. Simon was also recognized as high priest by the people, but he and his two sons were eventually murdered.

In 134 B.C., John Hyrcanus I became the head of state and ruled until 104 B.C., and the Hasmonean dynasty continued after him until the time of Herod the Great, the son of Antipater of Idumea, who ruled from 37 to 4 B.C. The Roman occupation of Palestine began in 63 B.C., when Pompey led his army into Jerusalem and entered the Temple. With the aid of the Romans, Herod the Great began to reign in Judea.

When the Hasideans emerged in the course of the Maccabean Revolt, they did not espouse Jewish nationalism, but were zealous for the observance of the Mosaic Law and allegiance to the Zadokite priesthood. Consequently, they eventually broke with the Maccabean movement because of its nationalistic and political character. This break then gave rise to the Essenes, who may be regarded as the descendants of those Hasideans. Recall also the explanation of *Essēnoi* as "pious ones," the same meaning as the Hebrew name *Ḥăsîdîm*, "Hasideans." Moreover, it is significant that the earliest mention of the Essenes in Josephus's account is in the reign of Jonathan, the youngest son of Mattathias (*Ant.* 13.5.9 §171). So according to this Palestinian or Judean context, the Essenes emerged in Jewish history from the Hasidic movement about 150 B.C. This emergence is supported by evidence in the first column of the Damascus Document, which reads:

> In the period of wrath, three hundred and ninety years after He delivered them into the hands of Nebuchadnezzar, the king of Babylon, He visited them and made a shoot of planting sprout from Israel and from Aaron to take possession of His land and to grow rich with the good produce of His land. Then they came to realize their iniquity and to know that they were guilty people. They were like blind people and those groping for a path for over twenty years. Then God appraised their deeds, that they were seeking Him with undivided heart. So He raised up for them a Teacher of Righteousness to make them tread in the path of His heart, and to inform the last generations about what He would do in the final generation against the congregation of traitors. (CD 1:5-12)

The number "390" is a symbolic allusion to Ezek 4:5, and so it cannot be taken literally; but it might measure roughly the time from the Exile to Antiochus IV Epiphanes. In any case, the account about the rise of the Teacher of Righteousness thus anchors the emergence of the Essene community from the Hasidic movement about the middle of the second century B.C.[5] This explanation of the origin of the Essenes is held by the majority of scholars who interpret the QL today.

(2) *Babylonian Background.* This theory explains the origin of the Jewish sect of the Essenes as the remnant of Jews who had been

in exile at the time of the Babylonian Captivity (587–539 B.C.), brought there by Nebuchadnezzar, king of Babylon, after he devastated Judah and Jerusalem. Crucial to this explanation is the interpretation of the phrase *šābê Yiśrā'ēl* in CD 6:5, *šābê Yiśrā'ēl hayyôṣě'îm mē'ereṣ Yěhûdāh wayyāgûrû bā'ereṣ Dammeśeq*. Whereas most scholars who were studying QL interpreted the phrase as "the penitents (*or* converts) of Israel," S. Iwry[6] and J. Murphy-O'Connor[7] insisted that it means "the returnees to Israel," that is, those who returned to Israel from Babylon in the early second century after the year 167 B.C. This explanation appeals mainly to CD 6:2–11, which reads as follows:

> God recalled the covenant of the forefathers. He raised up from Aaron men of discernment and from Israel men of wisdom and made them listen. They dug the Well: "A well that princes dug, that nobles of the people delved with a staff" (Num 21:18). The Well is the Law, and those who dug it are the returnees to Israel (*šābê Yiśrā'ēl*) who went out from the land of Judah and resided in the land of Damascus. God called all of them princes, because they sought Him; and their fame has not been disputed by anyone. The Staff is the Interpreter of the Law, of whom Isaiah spoke: "He produces an instrument for his deeds" (54:16). But the nobles of the people are those who come to dig the well with the staves that the Staff provided: to conduct themselves during the whole age of wickedness, and without which they would not succeed, until there arises one who teaches righteousness at the end of days.

In this paragraph, "Damascus" is used as a code word for Babylon, as in Amos 5:26–27, which is quoted in CD 6:14–15, "I will send into exile the Sakkuth of your king and the Kiwan of your images away from my tents to Damascus." Cf. Ezra 2:1; Neh 7:6: "These were the people who came up out of the exile that Nebuchadnezzar, king of Babylon, had carried off; they returned to Jerusalem and Judah, each to his town." Cf. CD 4:2, "Here are the priests, the returnees to Israel who went out from the land of

Judah, and the levites are those who joined them....Look, this is the exact statement of their names according to their genealogies, the trials through which they passed, and the years of their sojourn in exile."

Moreover, one must recall that Josephus mentions that the Essenes were "of Jewish birth" (*Ioudaioi men genos ontes, J.W.* 2.8.2 §119). That implies that they were Jews of a distinct origin, different from the Pharisees and Sadducees that he has just named in the same paragraph, since it is inexplicable why Josephus would say this, if the Essenes were coming from a Judean background.

Likewise, the remnants of two rule books have been found in various Qumran caves, which are similar in many respects despite their differences in detail, suggesting that there were Essenes of different origins. Those who lived at Qumran seem to have lived according to the so-called Manual of Discipline (1QS, 4QS, etc.), whereas those who lived elsewhere, in the towns and villages through Judea, as Josephus records (*J.W.* 2.8.4 §124), probably used the Damascus Document (CD, 4QD). This writing may even have been composed (or at least begun) in Babylon, because the legislation in CD is not related at all to Pharisaic (or the later rabbinic) legislation but reflects a gentile environment in which the Jews for whom it was written were at that time living.

Such Jews, having heard about the success of the Maccabean Revolt, would have returned to Israel from their Babylonian abode, but when they saw what had become of Judaism and Jewish life in Israel as a result of the attempt to hellenize it, their conservative instincts would have moved some of them to withdraw to a solitary existence and insist on "the exact interpretation of the Law" (CD 4:8; 6:18–20), because they "had entered the new covenant in the land of Damascus" (ibid.).

Hence, according to this explanation, the Essene sect did not originate as a reaction to the hellenization of Judah under Antiochus IV Epiphanes, but "as the result of inspired reflection on the causes of the divine punishment that was the Exile."[8] Even though this explanation is not favored by many scholars who study the QL today, it is not easily dismissed.

History of the Essene Community

The Jews who belonged to the Essene movement were of four sorts: (1) the cenobitic Jews of the Qumran area; (2) those who lived in Jerusalem and other towns and villages of Judea; (3) those still in the camps of "the land of Damascus" (= Babylon); (4) the Therapeutae in Egypt, related to the Essenes of Judea. Here I shall concentrate mainly on the cenobites of the Qumran area.

From the archaeological evidence at Khirbet Qumran, it is clear that the Essenes began to occupy the community center in Phase Ib, about the time that John Hyrcanus I was king and high priest in Judea (134–104 B.C.). Prior to that time, when they withdrew to Qumran, they were a disorganized group, such as described in the Damascus Document, "In the period of wrath, three hundred and ninety years after He delivered them into the hands of Nebuchadnezzar, the king of Babylon, He visited them and made a shoot of planting sprout from Israel and Aaron to take possession of His land" (CD 1:5–8). The Manual of Discipline narrates how the community began:

> When these people become a community in Israel according to these rules, they will separate from the habitation of sinful people to go into the desert to open the way of Him, as it stands written, "In the desert, prepare the way of ••••, make straight in the wilderness a path for our God" (Isa 40:3). This (path) is the study of the Law, which He prescribed through Moses, that they are to do according to all that has been revealed from age to age, as the prophets have made known by His holy Spirit. (1QS 8:12–16)

The Damascus Document further records that in the beginning the members of the new covenant were "like blind people and those groping for a path for over twenty years" before God "raised up for them a Teacher of Righteousness" (CD 1:9–11). This means that at the outset the community was a rather amorphous group with little or no leadership. Indeed, an apostasy even occurred within the group, as the same document records: "Thus, all the men who entered the new covenant in the land of Damascus and who returned, then betrayed (it) and departed from the Well of living waters, shall not be counted in the assembly of the people" (CD 19:33–35). This text also implies that there were some Essenes who did not return to Judea and were still in Babylon.

The ultra-conservatism of those who did return did not allow them to worship in the Jerusalem Temple or take part in its sacrifices because of their commitment to the Zadokite line of priests and the use of a different calendar. The Damascus Document again records: "All those who have been admitted to the covenant shall not enter the Temple to kindle His altar in vain....They shall take care to act according to the exact interpretation of the Law during the age of wickedness: to keep apart from the children of the pit, to keep far from evil wealth that defiles, either by promise or vow, and from the wealth of the Temple, and from stealing from the poor of His people..." (CD 6:11–16). Josephus likewise records this attitude to Temple sacrifices: "They send votive offerings to the Temple, but offer no sacrifices, using a different ritual of purification. Consequently, they are barred from those areas of the Temple that are frequented by all the people, and offer their sacrifices elsewhere by themselves" (*Ant.* 18.1.5 §19). All of these details explain why the Essenes were like "blind people" during the first 20 years.

In this situation, the Teacher of Righteousness (*môrēh haṣṣedeq*) appeared, raised by God to lead the Essenes and to instruct them (CD 1:11). He was a priest (1QpHab 2:7–8), of the Zadokite line, and not one of the Hasmonean line that was serving then in the Jerusalem Temple. Unfortunately, one cannot identify the historical person who bears this name, possibly because "the city was without a high priest for seven years," as Josephus records (*Ant.* 20.10.3 §237). In the *Hodayot* (Thanksgiving Psalms), some of the hymns are composed in the first person singular ("I give you thanks, Lord, that You..."), and many commentators think that they were composed by the Teacher of Righteousness himself. If that is true, one can cull from them details about the life of the Teacher: that God endowed him with many blessings in his childhood (1QH^a 17 [old 9]:29–32, 34–36); that he was, with God's grace, a man of high moral character (1QH^a 6 [old 14]:17–19); that God had accorded him knowledge and insight into divine mysteries (1QH^a 12 [old 4]:5–6; 15 [old 7]:26–27); that he has been unjustly persecuted (1QH^a 12 [old 4]:8–11); that God has given him endurance in the time of such persecution (1QH^a 13 [old 5]:11–18).

The Teacher of Righteousness was the leader of many of the community who were also priests of the Zadokite line (*bĕnê Ṣādôq*, "sons of Zadok"), as well as of many more who were not priests, to whom reference is often made in the QL as "the Many" (*hā-rabbîm*), whom he taught to be worthy members of the New Covenant in the land of Israel.

It was not long, however, before an opponent of the Teacher of Righteousness appeared on the scene, an individual who is called in various Qumran texts "the Wicked Priest" (*hakkôhēn hārāšāʿ*, 1QpHab 1:[13]; 11:4; 12:2). He is not otherwise identified, but many commentators maintain that his title in such texts is a play on his real title (*hakkôhēn hā-rōʾš*, "the high priest") and that he was Jonathan, son of Mattathias, one of the Maccabees (160–142 B.C.). When Jonathan became the leader in Israel, he reigned for eight years with no official title. He was appointed high priest by the Seleucid ruler, Alexander Balas, in 152 B.C. (1 Macc 10:20), and two years later was nominated ethnarch, the civil and military governor of Judea; but it would be more accurate to say that he usurped the high priestly office, started the Hasmonean priesthood, and sought to remove the Zadokite line of priests. Because of this usurpation, he was called by the Essenes "the Wicked Priest" and was regarded as the opponent of the Teacher of Righteousness: "the Wicked Priest, who persecuted the Teacher of Righteousness to do away with him in the heat of his wrath in the abode of his retreat. On a feast day, during the rest of the Day of Atonement, he appeared to them to do away with them and to make them stumble on the fast-day, the sabbath of their rest" (1QpHab 11:4–8). From this passage one learns that the Teacher of Righteousness and his followers were living somewhere outside of Jerusalem in a place of exile or retreat (probably Qumran); but also that the Essenes and the Jerusalem priest were following different calendars. For on such a feast day as the Day of Atonement, Jews were permitted to travel or walk only a short distance. Hence, the Day of Atonement, as observed by the Teacher of Righteousness and his followers, must have been a different day from that observed by the Wicked Priest, who made his way to the dwelling place of the Essenes.

The same document relates what happened to the Wicked Priest, who persecuted the Essenes and their Teacher: "...the Wicked Priest, whom, because of the evil done to the Teacher of Righteousness and the members of his party, God delivered into the hands of his enemies to punish him with cruel blows (and) destroy him in bitterness of soul for having done evil to His chosen ones" (1QpHab 9:9–12). So the Wicked Priest suffered a terrible death. Josephus reports that Jonathan died at the hands of the Syrian Tryphon (*Ant.* 13.6.6 §209), and this is another reason for thinking that Jonathan was the Wicked Priest. Further allusion to this death of Jonathan is made in 4QpPs[a] (4Q171) 3–10:8–10.

The Essene community continued to thrive at Qumran all during Phase Ib of its occupation, when its numbers increased. This was so especially in the time of Herod the Great (37–4 B.C.), whom the Essenes favored as the ruler, because during his reign the Hasmonean dynasty began to lose power. The Essenes continued to be hostile to the current priesthood in Jerusalem and the lay teachers of the Law, who followed a different tradition of interpreting it.

By this time the Teacher of Righteousness must have died, because there is no longer any mention of him in documents from this period. This phase came to an end in 31 B.C., when an earthquake wreaked havoc in many parts of the construction that the Essenes had erected there (Josephus, *Ant.* 15.5.2 §121). Whether the community continued to live there after that disaster is disputed. De Vaux maintained that the Essenes then migrated to Damascus and did not return to Qumran until 4 B.C., but Milik, Magness, and others have questioned that migration.[9] In any case, Phase Ib of Essene existence at Qumran then came to an end. When Herod the Great died in 4 B.C., Judea entered a period of chaos, as many citizens opposed the continuation of his dynasty; war broke out and the Romans sent troops into Judea to pacify the country.

The Essene community resumed dwelling at Qumran after the earthquake, and this period became known as Phase II, when some of the dilapidated buildings were restored. Though new recruits joined them, they were not as numerous as in Phase Ib. The Essenes then became more opposed to the Roman occupation of Judea, as they developed an eschatological view of their existence. They not only looked forward to the coming of a Prophet and the Messiahs of Aaron and Israel (1QS 9:11), but fostered a warlike tendency like that of the Zealots. The War Scroll (1QM) gives evidence of this attitude, as it describes a war in the end-time that God was going to engage in with His angels on the side of "the sons of light" (the Essenes) against "the sons of darkness" (the Kittim [a code name for the Romans] and all others who did not agree with the "sons of light"). Despite this Zealot tendency, the Essenes continued to live there according to their usual way of life, until the Roman Legio X Fretensis captured the site and burnt the community center in the summer of A.D. 68.

Before the Roman soldiers arrived, however, the sectarians at Qumran managed to deposit their scrolls in caves that they had hollowed out on the southern edge of the plateau, where they lay for centuries until A.D. 1952, when they were discovered in what came to be known as Caves 4, 5, and 6. Some of the Essenes undoubtedly died at the hands of the Romans and were buried in the nearby cemetery. What happened to the rest of them after that destruction is not known; that is the story for chap. XIV of this book.

Roman soldiers, however, occupied part of the community center for a few years, before it was abandoned. Some monks reused part of the buildings in Byzantine times. Then it lay in ruins until the discovery of the Qumran Scrolls and the excavation of the site.

Organization of the Essene Community

This group of ancient Palestinian Jews was quite different from their contemporaries, especially from the Pharisees and the Sadducees. Even before the Qumran Scrolls were discovered, the ancient sources that I have mentioned already noted the distinctive character of the Essenes. Even the Roman writer Pliny the Elder called attention to their common life, their celibacy, and their nonuse of money. Now that two of their rule books have been found in Qumran caves, the Manual of Discipline (1QS) and the Damascus Document (CD), even though they differ in details, many features of the Essene common life are known. Thus, much of the evidence about it is firsthand, and not simply from extrinsic sources.

Four aspects of the Essene community and its organization have to be considered: (1) aim and purpose; (2) rule books; (3) membership; and (4) reception of candidates.

(1) *Aim and Purpose*. The noble purpose of the Essene community is expressed well in the opening paragraph of the Manual of Discipline, which reads:

> ...the rule of the community: to seek God with all one's heart and all one's soul, so as to do what is good and upright before Him, as He commanded through Moses and through all His servants the Prophets; to love all that He has chosen and to hate all that He has rejected; to abstain from all evil and to cling to all good deeds; to practise fidelity, righteousness, and justice in the land and to walk no more with a stubborn and guilty heart and lustful eyes committing every sort of evil; to welcome all who freely volunteer to carry out God's decrees in the covenant of kindness;...to love all the sons of light, each according to his lot in God's design and to hate all the sons of darkness, each according to his guilt in God's vengeance. (1QS 1:1–11; 4QS^a [4Q255] 1:1–6)

The purpose of the community is set forth again in 1QS 5:1–3, which reads:

> This is the rule for the men of the Community who freely volunteer to convert from all wickedness and to keep themselves steadfast in all that He has commanded, in accordance with His will. They shall keep apart from the assembly of men of iniquity in order to constitute a Community in law and possessions, and to submit to the authority of the sons of Zadok, the priests who safeguard the covenant and to the authority of the Many of the men of the Community, those who persevere rigorously in the covenant.

(2) *Rule Books.* Two rule books were found in the Qumran caves, the Manual of Discipline or *Serek Hayyaḥad,* "The Rule of the Community" (1QS), which came to light in Qumran Cave 1, with 10 or 11 copies of parts of it found in Cave 4 (4QS$^{a-j/k}$), a fragmentary copy from Cave 5 (5QS [5Q11]), and possibly another related text (5Q13); and the Damascus Document (CD) or Zadokite Document, which was found in Egypt and has been known since 1896, but which is related to the Qumran Scrolls, because fragmentary copies of it were retrieved from Caves 4 (4QD^{a-h} [4Q266–273]), 5 (5QD [5Q12]), and 6 (6QD [6Q15]).

(a) *The Rule of the Community.* 1QS is a full copy of the rule, having 11 columns, and written in Hasmonean script, dated to 100–75 B.C.[10] For many scholars who have been studying the QL, 1QS is the rule book of the Essenes at Qumran.

After the introduction (1:1–15), which states the aim and purpose of the community (see above), it has six parts:

(i) the rite for entrance into the covenant, the ceremony, and a denunciation of those who refuse to enter (1:16—3:12)
(ii) the theological tenets of the community and its doctrine of the two spirits (3:13—4:26)
(iii) another statement of the purpose of the community and various of its rules (5:1—6:23)
(iv) the penal code of the community (6:24—7:25)
(v) description of the model, pioneer community (8:1—9:26)
(vi) the hymns of the community's worship service (10:1—11:22)

This rule hardly was written all at one time; its repetitions, additions, and omissions, which become obvious when 1QS is studied along with the fragments from Caves 4 and 5, reveal that it is a composite text, put together at various times.[11]

Two important appendices of 1QS are extant, "The Rule of the Congregation" (*serek lĕkûl 'ădat Yiśrā'ēl,* lit., "the rule of the whole congregation of Israel"), 1QSa (1Q28a); and a "Collection of Blessings" (*dibrê bĕrākāh,* lit., "words of a blessing"), 1QSb

THE MANUAL OF DISCIPLINE, (1QS),
THE RULE BOOK FOR THE COMMUNITY

(1Q28b).[12] The Rule of the Congregation sets forth instructions for new members of the community (including women and children); rules for troops; rules for special groups (old men, mentally unbalanced, Levites); rule for the meeting of the whole community; and order of the messianic assembly and banquet. The Collection of Blessings supplies the way the Sage (*maśkîl*) is to bless the faithful of the community (i.e., the ordinary members), to bless the chief priest of the community, and to bless the other priests along with the Prince of the Congregation.

(b) *Damascus Document.* The Cairo Genizah copy of this rule book, which does not contain the whole text, exists in two manuscripts: manuscript A^1 (containing 1:1—8:21, written on both sides of four sheets), and A^2 (containing 9:1—16:20, written in the same way but in a different script). Both parts are dated palaeographically: manuscript A to the tenth century A.D.; and manuscript B (containing 19:1—20:34, written on both sides of one sheet), dated to the twelfth century A.D. Part of B overlaps parts of A.[13] Other fragmentary copies of the Damascus Document have been found in Caves 4 (4QD^{a-h} [4Q266–273]),[14] 5 (5QD [5Q12]), 6 (6QD [6Q15]).[15] This document probably represents the rule book of Essenes living not at Qumran but elsewhere throughout Judea, since it speaks of them living in "camps" (*maḥănôt*, CD 7:6; 10:23;

12:23). This document has three main parts: (a) An exhortation (found in some 4QD texts, CD 1:1—8:21 [=CD 19:1—20:34]); (b) Legal prescriptions (missing from CD, but found in some 4QD texts); (c) Constitution: Life in the New Covenant (found in CD 15:1—16:20; then in CD 9:1—14:22 [the order of this part is known from 4QD^e]).

Because many fragmentary copies of CD were found in the Qumran caves along with many copies of 1QS, the two rule books were related clearly to the same Jews in Judea, despite the difference in details that they have.

(3) *Membership.* Members of the Essene community were convinced that they were the Israel of the end-time, and they tried to model themselves after Israel described in the Book of Numbers, meaning that they were divided into tribes, thousands, hundreds, fifties, and tens (1QS 2:19–22). At the core of the community were "the sons of Zadok, the priests" (*běnê Ṣādôq hakkôhănîm*) as the Appendix of the Manual of Discipline (1QSa [1Q28a]) puts it: "...they gather in community to walk according to the regulations of the sons of Zadok, the priests, the men of the covenant, who have turned away from the path of the (rest of the) people" (1:1–2). The priests were assisted by the Levites (*hal-Lěwiyîm* of the community (1QS 2:4); for instance, when the priests utter the blessings, the Levites utter the curses.

The Zadokite priests then assemble others, that is, the lay members (sometimes called generically "Israel"); they are broken down accordingly into: (a) the youths (*hanně'ārîm*), who have to be educated and instructed for 10 years in the precepts of the covenant and the "Book of Meditation" (*sēpher he-hŏgî* [1QSa 1:6–8]); (b) the enrolled (*happěqûdîm*), those 20 years of age, who thus are admitted to the holy community (1:9–12); (c) the foundations of the holy congregation (*yěsôdôt 'ădat haqqôdeš*), that is, the officials, who have to be at least 25 years old (1:12–13); (d) those advanced in years (*běrôbôt šěnê 'îš*). To all of these, tasks are assigned according to their abilities by the priests, and they work in the service of the tribes and families, who are gathered in thousands, hundreds, fifties, and tens (1:19—2:1).

However, "no man smitten with any human uncleanness shall enter God's assembly....No man smitten in his flesh, or paralyzed

40

in feet or hands, no lame or blind or deaf or dumb,...no old and tottery man unable to stand still...shall hold any office in the congregation of the men of renown, for holy angels are with their congregation" (1QSa 2:4–10). This strange regulation is supposed probably to prevent God's holy angels from having to gaze on such human imperfections.

It is to be noted that no women or children are mentioned in 1QS as members of the Essene community at Qumran; but they are included in the Appendix (1QSa) and seem to be in CD.

The Essene community recognized the authority of a Superintendent, *hammĕbaqqēr ʿal hārabbîm*, lit., "Overseer over the Many" (1QS 6:12; cf. 6:20). In the Damascus Document, he is called rather *hammĕbaqqēr ʾăšer lĕkol hammaḥănôt*, "Overseer of all the camps" (CD 14:8–12). There was also a "Community Council" (*ʿăṣat hayyaḥad*), which was comprised of "twelve laymen and three priests" (1QS 8:1); they probably symbolized the twelve tribes of Israel and three priestly families descended from Levi through Gershon, Kohath, and Merari. Instead of such a council, there was, in the camps of which the Damascus Document speaks, a group of "ten judges" (*šōpĕṭê hāʿēdāh ʿad ʿăśārāh ʾănāšîm*, lit., "judges of the congregation up to ten men ("four from the tribe of Levi and Aaron, and six from Israel" [CD 10:4–5]).

(4) *Reception of Candidates.* One was not a member of the Essene community simply because one was a Jew. The Manual of Discipline mentions frequently those who "freely offer themselves" (1QS 1:7, 11; 5:1, 6, 8, 10, 21, 22), using a verb that means "offer voluntarily": one had to apply for membership, then submit to periods of training before one was admitted fully into the community. The same manual describes the process of reception:

> As for anyone from Israel who would freely offer himself to enroll in the council of the Community, the Deputy at the head of the Many shall examine him concerning his insight and his deeds. If he passes muster for the discipline, he shall admit him into the Covenant, so that he can turn to the truth and turn away from all iniquity. He shall instruct him in all the precepts of the Community. Later, when he comes to stand before the Many, they

shall inquire about everything concerning his affairs. As a decision is made according to the counsel of the Many, he shall enter or withdraw. When he enters the council of the Community, he must not touch the Purity of the Many, until they examine him about his spirit and his deeds at the completion of a full year. Nor shall he share in the property of the Many. On his completion of a year, the Many shall make inquiry into his affairs, into his insight and his observance of the Law. If the decision favors him, according to the word of the priests and the majority of the men of the Covenant, to enter the core of the Community, his property and his earnings (shall be given) to the Overseer over the revenues of the Many; and it shall be credited to his account, but he [i.e., the Overseer] shall not use it on behalf of the Many. He [i.e., the candidate] must not touch the Drink of the Many, until his completion of a second year among the men of the Community. On his completion of this second year, they shall examine him. According to the word of the Many, if the decision favors him to enter the Community, they shall inscribe him in the order of his rank among his brothers, in what concerns the Law, equity, the Purity, and the mingling of his property. His counsel and his judgment shall be for the Community. (1QS 6:13–23)

From this passage we learn that the candidate had a year of postulancy (to use the terminology of modern religious congregations), during which he had to live according to the community's regulations. Then there was a two-year novitiate before he was admitted fully into the community; after the first year, he could take part in some of its features. At the end of the second year, the candidate became a full member and partook of the community's "Purity." This term means the meal that was taken in common by the Many; a description of which is found in 1QSa (1Q28a) 2:11–22:

At a session of the men of renown, those called to the feast for the Community council, when God will beget

42

the Messiah among them, the Priest shall enter at the head of all the congregation of Israel, and all his brothers, the sons of Aaron, the priests, called to the feast, as men of renown, shall sit before him, each according to his dignity. Afterwards, the Messiah of Israel shall enter; and all the heads of the Thousands of Israel shall sit before him, each according to his dignity, according to his standing in their camps and marches. All the heads of the households of the congregation, their sages [ ] shall sit before them, each according to his dignity. When they gather at the table of the Community or to drink new wine, and the communal table is set and the new wine is mixed for drinking, no one shall stretch forth his hand to the firstfruits of the bread and the new wine before the Priest. For he shall bless the firstfruits of the bread and the wine; and shall stretch forth his hand to the bread before them. Afterwards, the Messiah of Israel shall stretch forth his hand to the bread. Then all the congregation of the Community shall bless, each one according to his dignity. In accordance with this statute, they shall act at every meal, when at least ten members are gathered.

What is noteworthy in this description is the presence of the Messiah of Israel at the common meal and of the precedence given to the Priest over the Messiah.

Finally, when the candidate became a full member of the community, he had to turn over all his property to it. "If anyone is found among them who has lied knowingly about his possessions, he shall be excluded from the Purity of the Many for a year, and they shall withhold a quarter of his food" (1QS 6:24–25).

IV

THE LANGUAGES OF
THE SCROLLS

Being documents of ancient Jews living in Judea in the last pre-Christian centuries and during the first century A.D., the Qumran Scrolls were written in three languages, Hebrew, Aramaic, and Greek. Each of these languages appears in forms that were little known prior to the discovery of the scrolls.

(1) *Hebrew*. The vast majority of the texts retrieved from the Qumran caves were written in Hebrew. The various biblical texts discovered there were copied in the consonantal form of Biblical Hebrew that was characteristic of the given book, either preexilic or postexilic Biblical Hebrew. At times, however, these copies display the fuller spelling found in many other Qumran Hebrew texts, for example, *qwdš* (= *qôdeš*) instead of merely *qdš* (pronounced in the same way). That fuller spelling is called *scriptio plena*, which means the use of certain consonants to indicate vowels (e.g., *aleph* or *hē* for *a*; *waw* for *u* or *ô*; *yodh* for *î*); such consonants were called *matres lectionis* (lit., "mothers of a reading").

The nonbiblical Qumran texts, however, were written in a consonantal form of Hebrew that is later than the postexilic biblical form but not identical to what was used in the earliest of the rabbinical writings, known as Mishnaic Hebrew, which is a form of the language that appears about A.D. 200–220. Many of the sectarian and parabiblical literary writings used by the Essenes were composed in Qumran Hebrew.[1] This is strange, because at that time most of the Jews in Judea would have been speaking Aramaic. It is often thought that the Essenes resuscitated the use of spoken Hebrew because it was regarded by them as *lěšôn haqqōdeš*, "the language of the Sanctuary."

Many nonbiblical texts, written in Qumran Hebrew, are the originals of writings previously known only in ancient translations, such as Ethiopic or Greek. For instance, the *Book of Jubilees* was read only in Ethiopic prior to the discovery of the Hebrew texts 1QJub^{a-b} (1Q17–18), 2QJub^{a-b} (2Q19–20), 3QJub (3Q5), 4QJub$^{a, c-g}$ (4Q216, 218–222), 11QJub (11Q12).

(2) *Aramaic.* Aramaic is a sister language of Hebrew, using the very same consonants but vocalizing them differently. For instance, "the king" would be *hammélek* in Hebrew, but *malkā'* in Aramaic, having the same three consonants, *mlk*, the root of the verb "to rule, reign." Qumran Aramaic, however, is a form of the language later than Biblical Aramaic but not identical to the form that appears later in rabbinic writings of the fourth century A.D. Some fragments of Daniel and Ezra from the Qumran caves preserve the Biblical Aramaic form of those biblical books, but often with fuller spelling. Four of the five texts of Tobit were composed in the Qumran form of Aramaic (4QTob^{a-d} [4Q196–199]). *Enoch* was known only in Ethiopic and Greek (*1 Enoch*) prior to the discovery of the Aramaic texts: 1QEnGiants^{a-b} (1Q23–24), 2QEnGiants (2Q26), 4QEn^{a-g} (4Q201–202, 204–207, 212), 4QEnastr^{a-d} (4Q208–211), 4QEnGiants^{a-c} (4Q203, 530–533).

What is most important in this case are the targums found in some Qumran caves. A targum is an Aramaic translation of the Hebrew text of a biblical book, and many of them exist from later times in the Christian period. Originally, the targum was recited orally by an interpreter in the Jewish synagogue after a corresponding biblical passage had been read in Hebrew. However, there are now two copies of the targum of Job (4QtgJob [4Q157]; 11QtgJob [11Q10]), and one of the targum of Leviticus (4QtgLev [4Q156]). These texts are important because they show that targums were being written down already in pre-Christian times, whereas it was often thought that it was forbidden then to put them in writing.[2]

(3) *Greek.* Although most of the writings found in the Qumran caves were composed in a Semitic language, either Hebrew or Aramaic, some were discovered that were written in Greek These include texts of the Septuagint, that is, the translation of the Hebrew OT into Hellenistic Greek: 4QLXXLev^{a} gr (4Q119); 4QLXXNum gr (4Q121); 4QLXXDeut gr (4Q122); and all the

fragmentary texts from Qumran Cave 7 (7Q1–19), two of which are biblical (7QExod gr [7Q1] and 7QEpJer gr [7Q2]). The rest of the fragments of Cave 7 have been controversial, because it was claimed that most of them actually were of NT writings (see p. 96 below).

The mode of writing in which the Hebrew and Aramaic languages of the Qumran texts were composed is called the "Aramaic Square Script," which was in common use in Judea at that time. On occasion, however, the Qumran scribes used a more ancient script called "paleo-Hebrew," especially when it was necessary to write the name of God, YHWH (Yahweh), the tetragrammaton (four-letter name). The name so written is found often in a text that is otherwise composed in the Aramaic Square Script. Moreover, there is one document in which the entire Hebrew text is so written, the Leviticus scroll from Qumran Cave 11 (11QpaleoLev).

V

THE SCRIPTURES IN THE SCROLLS:
Old Testament, Targums, Canon

The discovery of copies of the Hebrew Scriptures in the Qumran caves gives concrete evidence of what Josephus wrote about the Essenes' esteem for Moses and his writings: "After God, they hold most in esteem the name of their lawgiver, any blasphemer of whom is put to death" (*J.W.* 2.8.9 §145). Moreover, the Qumran copies have revolutionized not only the critical study of those biblical writings (i.e., textual criticism), but also the study of the canon and ancient translations (in Aramaic, Greek, and Latin). They have proved to be so important because, before they were discovered, the oldest manuscript of a Hebrew biblical text, the Ben Asher Codex of the Prophets, was dated to A.D. 895.[1] The manuscript of Isaiah from Qumran Cave 1 (1QIsa^a) is dated 125–100 B.C. and is roughly a thousand years older than the Ben Asher Codex.

Most of the biblical texts have been inscribed on animal skin (of a lamb or a kid), which was prepared for writing in the basins of 'Ain Feshkha. Some texts of Kings, Daniel, and Tobit are found on papyrus, which may have come from reeds grown locally or from Lake Huleh in Galilee. The skin was inscribed usually on the hair side. The work of copying the biblical texts was carried out by Essene scribes in the scriptorium of the main Qumran building, where a writing bench and inkwells have been found.

1. Biblical Books in Hebrew

The majority of the biblical books written in Hebrew were found in Qumran Cave 4, but Caves 1–3, 5–8, and 11 also yielded a goodly number of them. All told, they number about 202, a little less than a quarter of all the texts retrieved from the 11 Qumran caves. Almost 20 more come from other sites, such as Murabba'at and Masada. Most of the documents are fragmentary, but a complete copy of all 66 chapters of the Book of Isaiah was among the seven big texts from Qumran Cave 1 (1QIsa[a]), from which another sizable, but not complete, copy was retrieved (1QIsa[b]). The only books not represented among the fragments are Esther and Nehemiah. There is, however, a fragmentary text of Ezra (4QEzra [4Q117]), which may offset the loss of Nehemiah, because in antiquity Ezra and Nehemiah were considered at times as one writing.

From the 11 Qumran caves have come the following number of texts for the various books of the OT:

Genesis	19–20 (including two that are Genesis-Exodus)
Exodus	14
Leviticus	9 (including one that is Leviticus-Numbers)
Numbers	5–6
Deuteronomy	27
Joshua	2
Judges	3
1–2 Samuel	4
1–2 Kings	3
Isaiah	20–24
Jeremiah	6
Ezekiel	6
Twelve Prophets	8
Psalms	34
Proverbs	2
Job	4
Ruth	4
Canticles	4

Lamentations	4
Qoheleth	2–3
Daniel	8
Ezra	1
1–2 Chronicles	1

These numbers vary, when one compares them with other lists that are given at times, because some copies are so small and difficult to read that not everyone identifies them the same way. The list shows the books of the Hebrew Scriptures that were most popular among the Qumran Essenes: the Psalms, Genesis, Deuteronomy, and Isaiah.

Many of these biblical texts were copied by Essene scribes at Qumran, and often they can be detected by the distinctive mode of writing and spelling. Some texts are dated palaeographically to a time before the Essene community began to live at Qumran; they show that they were copied elsewhere and were brought to the desert retreat when the Essenes came there. Thus, the oldest text, 4QExod^f is dated 250 B.C. In general, the biblical texts reflect three of the scripts commonly used at Qumran: Archaic, Hasmonean, and Herodian. About a dozen of them, however, are written in a paleo-Hebrew script not otherwise attested in Qumran scrolls,[2] e.g., 4QpaleoGen-Exod^l (4Q11), 4QpaleoGen^m (4Q12), 4QpaleoDeut^r (4Q45), 4QpaleoJob^c (4Q101).

2. Biblical Books in Aramaic

The chapters of the Book of Daniel and of Ezra that are preserved in Aramaic in the Masoretic Text in use today are represented in fragmentary texts from Qumran: for example, 1QDan^a (1Q71), 1QDan^b (1Q72), 4QDan^a (4Q112), 4QDan^b (4Q113), 6QDan (6Q7), 4QEzra (4Q117). Some of these fragments have preserved the verses where the language changes from Hebrew, in which the beginning of the book of Daniel is composed, to Aramaic (Dan 2:4) and from Aramaic back to Hebrew (Dan 8:1—12:13), with which the book ends. Daniel is, then, a strange biblical book, being written in both Hebrew and Aramaic, and no one has been able to say why.

3. Biblical Books in Greek

A few fragments of the Greek translation of the Pentateuch, commonly known as the Old Greek or Septuagint version, have turned up in Qumran Cave 4: for example, 4QLXXLev^a gr (4Q119), which has the text of Lev 26:2–16; 4QLXXNum gr (4Q121), which has several verses from Numbers 3 and 4; 4QLXXDeut gr (4Q122), with Deut 11:4. It is puzzling that these Greek fragments are all from the Pentateuch, and none from any of the Prophets or the Writings.

4. Targums

As already explained, a targum is an Aramaic translation of a biblical Hebrew book. A few of such translations have been found in Qumran caves, which shows that written translations of Hebrew biblical books were already in existence in pre-Christian times. There are, for instance, the targum of Job, 4QtgJob (4Q157), which contains the Aramaic form of Job 3:5–9; 4:16—5:4 (dated to the first century A.D.); 11QtgJob (11Q10), which contains the Aramaic form of many passages from Job 17:14—42:12 (dated to the last half of the first century B.C.); and the targum of Leviticus (4QtgLev [4Q156]), which translates the Hebrew of Lev 16:12–15, 18–21 (dated to the second century B.C.).

5. Deuterocanonical Books

It is striking that not only texts of the protocanonical books of the OT have turned up in Qumran caves, but also some of the deuterocanical books. These are the Epistle of Jeremy (or Baruch 6), vv. 43–44 in pap7QLXXEpJer gr (7Q2); Sirach or the Wisdom of Ben Sira (often called Ecclesiasticus) 6:14–15?; 6:20–31 in 2QSir (2Q18), and Sir 51:13–20; 30 is found in 11QPsa (11Q5) 21:11–22:1.[3] Moreover, a good-sized copy of Sirach was found also at Masada, containing the Hebrew text of 39:27–32; 40:10–19, 26–30; 41:1–22; 42:1–25; 43:1–30.[4] Tobit, which was known mainly from

Greek translations prior to the Qumran discoveries, has been found in extensive fragments not only in Aramaic (4QTob^{a-d} [4Q196–199]), but also in Hebrew (4QTob^e [4Q200]).[5]

6. Phylacteries and Mezuzoth

The OT text is found in Qumran writings not only in the biblical scrolls but also in phylacteries and mezuzoth.

(a) A phylactery (*tĕphillah*) is a small box made of animal skin and containing parchment slips inscribed with Pentateuchal passages, which a Jewish man wears on his left arm and forehead as he recites his prayers, in accordance with Exod 13:9, 16 ("as a mark on your hand and frontlets between your eyes"). In Qumran Cave 4, 21 phylacteries were discovered (4Qphyl^{a-u} [4Q128–148]).[6] Others were found in Cave 1 (1Q13), Cave 5 (5Q8), and Cave 8 (8Q3). The Pentateuchal passages found on most of these Essene phylacteries are Deut 5:1—6:9; 10:21—11:21; Exod 12:43—13:16; Deut 32:14–20, 32–33 (the full text of these passages is not always copied).[7]

(b) A mezuzah (*mĕzûzāh*) is a small case, usually of metal, in which a small parchment inscribed with Deut 6:4–9 and 11:13–21 and the name *Šaddai*, "the Almighty," was inserted before the case was affixed to the doorpost of a Jewish house as a reminder of the faith of its inhabitants. In Qumran Cave 4, seven mezuzoth were discovered (4QMez^{a-g} [4Q149–155]),[8] and one from Cave 8 (8QMez [8Q4]). These Essene examples display a variety of Pentateuchal passages; each has to be examined for itself.

7. Textual Criticism

The greatest impact that the discovery of biblical texts in the Qumran caves has made is on the critical study of the Hebrew Scriptures. Emanuel Tov has summarized the contribution that the Qumran texts have made to biblical research.[9] For instance, he has emphasized readings previously unknown, which now enable one to understand better details in the traditional Masoretic Text that had been obscured by omissions.

SCROLLS ON DISPLAY AT QUMRAN EXHIBIT SITE

Tov has also shown how some of the Qumran biblical texts reveal the reliability of ancient translations, such as the Old Greek (or Septuagint), because some copies of the Hebrew text agree more with the Septuagint than with the traditional Masoretic Text. For instance, 4QExod^b (4Q13) has 23 variant readings that agree with the Old Greek, whereas 13 variants agree with the MT.[9] Similarly 4QDeut^q (4Q44) 5 ii 6–11[10], preserves a form of the Song of Moses (Deut 32:43) that is closer to the Old Greek than to the MT.[11]

Especially important in this regard are two texts of 1–2 Samuel from Cave 4: 4QSam^a (4Q51) and 4QSam^b (4Q52), for they have many readings that agree with the Septuagint more than with the Masoretic Text. They thus show that the Septuagint was a reliable translation of a Hebrew text that differed from the Masoretic. 4QSam^a (4Q51) also contains an important passage (10:6–9 [DJD 17. 65–66]) that is lacking in the Masoretic Text. It is part of the narrative about Nahash, the king of the Ammonites, and the verses omitted would be between 1 Sam 10:27 and 11:1. They run as follows:

> Naḥash, king of the Ammonites, oppressed the Gadites
> and the Reubenites with violence, and he gouged out
> every right eye of them and struck dread and terror in
> Israel. There was not left a man among the Israelites in
> Transjordan, whose right eye Naḥash, king of the
> Ammonites, had not gouged out. About seven thousand
> men fled from the Ammonites and came to Jabesh-
> gilead. It happened that about a month later 11:1
> Naḥash, the Ammonite, went up and besieged Jabesh-
> gilead, and all the men of Jabesh-gilead said to Naḥash,
> the Ammonite, "Make a pact with us, and we shall serve
> you." Naḥash, the Ammonite, said to them, "On this
> (condition) shall I make a pact with you...."

That such a passage would have been omitted from the Hebrew
text of 1 Samuel is striking indeed, but it shows the value of the
Qumran fragmentary biblical texts.

Important as such Hebrew texts are that agree more with the
Old Greek translation, there are, however, many others that do not.
Some of these manifest an affinity with the later Masoretic Text,
which, according to some scholars (F. M. Cross), is derived from a
scribal tradition dating from Babylon, where Jews were once in
exile. Still other Hebrew texts in the Qumran biblical collection
show a relation to the Samaritan Pentateuch, which was at home in
Palestine, whence the whole Pentateuch had its origin. These different geographical areas, Palestine, Egypt, and Babylon, are sepa-
rate; and so are the scribal traditions that result from them. This
has led some scholars, such as Cross, to explain the differences by
a "Theory of Local Texts." Tov, however, does not agree with such
an explanation, maintaining rather that the biblical texts of
Qumran are greatly diverse and manifest a textual plurality.

Apropos of textual criticism of the Hebrew biblical text, I
should point out that biblical fragments found in the caves of
Murabba'at, which date from the time of the Second Jewish Revolt
against Rome (roughly A.D. 130–135), are quite different from the
Qumran biblical texts. Such fragments have preserved a biblical text
that is almost identical with that of the later Masoretic Text of the
Pentateuch, Isaiah, the Psalms, and the Minor Prophets. The con-

trast between the Qumran biblical texts and these from Murabba'at reveals how important the former are, not only because of their age, but also because of the textual differences that they have.

8. Canon

This is a difficult topic to discuss, because "canon" is a Greek word (*kanōn*) that came to be used of authoritative biblical writings in the early Christian church. In the later rabbinical tradition, the idea of such writings was expressed by the formula, "writings that render the hands unclean": "The [Aramaic] version that is in Ezra and Daniel renders the hands unclean. If an [Aramaic] version [contained in the Scriptures] was written in Hebrew, or if [Scripture that is in] Hebrew was written in an [Aramaic] version, or in [paleo-] Hebrew script, it does not render the hands unclean" (*m. Yadaim* 4:5).

It is not known, however, whether there were such authoritative writings (or a canon of Scripture) in pre-Christian times or even how the Qumran Essenes then regarded such writings, which we call today apocryphal, deuterocanonical, or protocanonical writings. Even if one restricts the discussion to what now are called "biblical books," how many of the Qumran writings would fit into such a "canon," whether one speaks of the Catholic and Orthodox canon or the Protestant canon? If one could establish the Essene canon, would it apply to other Jewish people who were not Essenes?

In the NT, we come across the phrase "Moses and the Prophets" (Luke 16:29; 24:27) or "Moses and the Prophets and the Psalms" (Luke 24:44) or "the Law and the Prophets" (Matt 5:17; Acts 13:15) or "the Law of Moses and the Prophets" (Acts 28:23).[12] Commentators often have understood such phrases as indicating two or three parts of the canon of the OT and have argued that they show that there was already an awareness of a canon by the time the evangelists wrote. A similar phrase appears already in the prologue to the Wisdom of Ben Sira (or Sirach), "the Law and the Prophets and the Others that followed them." That prologue is dated 132 B.C., when the grandson of Ben Sira translated his grandfather's Hebrew writing into Greek.[13]

In QL, one finds formulas that reckon with different parts of the Hebrew Scriptures, but none of them has the succinctness of the NT expressions. Thus, God's commands have been given "through Moses and all His servants the Prophets" (1QS 1:3); "in the Book of Moses and in the books of the Prophets and in David" (4QMMT [4Q397] 14–21:10, 15 [without David]); "which Moses and Your servants, the Prophets, wrote" (4QDibHam[a] [4Q504] 1–2 iii 12–13); "(against) God's commands (given) through Moses and also through His holy Anointed Ones" (CD 5:21—6:1). These phrases, like that in Luke 24:44, reveal a growing awareness among the Essenes of Qumran of a third kind of authoritative writing that would eventually come to be called *Kětûbîm*, "Writings." These, along with *Tôrāh*, "Law," and *Něbî'îm*, "Prophets," thus reveal the growing awareness of authoritative writings that passed on the Word of God to His people, and this in a tripartite form. This would be the Essene idea of a "canon" of Scripture. The third form is confirmed by a prose insert called "David's Compositions" in 11QPs[a] 27:2–11. It precedes a quotation of Ps 140:1–5 and says that David composed 3,600 psalms and other songs to sing on different occasions. The sum total of them came to 4,050, and "all those he spoke in prophecy, which was given to him before the Most High."[14] This treatment of the Davidic Psalms does not constitute all of the "Writings," but it at least shows that there was an awareness of a set of authoritative writings different from the "Law" and "the Prophets," resulting in a tripartite division of a would-be canon.

VI

THE USE AND INTERPRETATION OF SCRIPTURE IN THE SECT

The Essenes differed from the Pharisees in that they did not have an oral tradition governing their understanding of the written Word of God. The Pharisaic oral tradition came to be called *tôrāh šebĕ'al peh*, "the Law according to the mouth," and differed from the *tôrāh šebiktāb*, "the Law that is in writing." The oral tradition of the Pharisees was written down eventually in the rabbinic period, about A.D. 200–220, under R. Judah Han-Naśi' (or Judah the Prince). That tradition thus began with the Mishnah and ended with the Talmuds, Palestinian and Babylonian. Lacking such an oral tradition, the Essenes resorted rather to a variety of ways of biblical exegesis or interpretation, among which the most important were written commentaries that they called *pĕšārîm*.

1. The Pesharim

The most distinctive use of Scripture by the Essenes was the pesher, "commentary." This literary genre was unknown before the discovery of the Qumran Scrolls. The name *pēšer* is derived from Qoh 8:1, "Who is like the sage, and who knows the interpretation of a word (*pēšer dābār*)?" The Aramaic form of the name, *pišrā'* occurs in Dan 2:4, where it supplies the interpretation or meaning of what has been seen in a dream.

This literary genre, related to the more generic sort called *midrāš*, "midrash, study," has as its starting point a biblical verse, usually drawn from one of the prophets or Psalms, which is quoted

56

and followed by *pišrô 'al...*, "the interpretation of it concerns...," or by *pēšer haddābār 'al...*, "the meaning of the word concerns." Then the interpretation or meaning supplied actualizes or contemporizes a person, an event, or a calendaric incident, for example, the Teacher of Righteousness, the Wicked Priest, the Day of Atonement. The mode of interpretation may be historical (referring to an event), allegorical (using symbolism), atomistic (analyzing letters of a word), paraphrastic (saying the same thing in other words), or eschatological (referring to the Essene idea of the end-time).

Scholars who have studied these texts sometimes divide them into three types: (a) historical, that is, relating to the history of the sect (e.g., 1QpHab, 1QpMic); (b) ethnic, that is, pertaining to the kinds of Jews in Judea (e.g., 4QpNah); (c) eschatological (e.g., the 4Q *pěšārîm* on Isaiah). Other scholars speak of continuous *pěšārîm*, that is, comments on one phrase or verse after another in a given biblical passage (e.g., 1QpHab, 4QpPs^a [from Psalm 37 to Psalm 45]) or thematic *pěšārîm*, that is, comments on a selected topic, with verses or phrases drawn from different unrelated biblical passages.

Eighteen Qumran fragmentary texts are *pěšārîm*: six using verses from Isaiah (3QpIsa [3Q4], 4QpIsa^a [4Q161], 4QpIsa^b [4Q162], 4QpIsa^c [4Q163], 4QpIsa^d [4Q164], 4QpIsa^e [4Q165]); two from Hosea (4QpHos^a [4Q166], 4QpHos^b [4Q167]); two from Micah (1QpMic [1Q14], 4QpMic [4Q168]); one from Nahum (4QpNah [4Q169]); one from Habakkuk (1QpHab); two from Zephaniah (1QpZeph [1Q15], 4QpZeph [4Q170]); one from Malachi (5QpMal [5Q10]); three from the Psalms (1QpPs [1Q16], 4QpPs^a [4Q171], 4QpPs^b [4Q173]). The copies of these *pěšārîm* are all dated in the first Christian century. There are, moreover, no multiple copies of such writings; so they represent the sole witnesses of such compositions. (Hence the superscript a and b used in the sigla above simply designate different copies of a commentary on a prophet or psalm, not multiple copies of the same commentary.)

A good example of a continuous pesher is the Pesher on Habakkuk (1QpHab), which comments on the text of Habakkuk chaps. 1 and 2 after citing its various verses. Habakkuk was a seventh-century prophet, who announced to the people of Judah that God was permitting the Chaldeans (from Babylonia) to invade their land and punish them because of their infidelity to Him. In his prophecy, Habakkuk describes the might of the coming invaders; but then he complains to God on behalf of the people of Judah. God answers the prophet, recounting how the Chaldeans will be punished. In the Qumran pesher, the author cites the various verses of Habakkuk 1—2 and interprets the words and phrases: the Chaldeans become the Kittim (the code name for the Romans then occupying contemporary Judea). For example,

> "Then the wind changes and sweeps on, and this one makes of his might his god" [Hab 1:11]. Its meaning concerns the leaders of the Kittim, who on the advice of the House of Guilty People pass by, one in front of the other; one after another, their leaders will come to devastate the land. (1QpHab 4:9–11)

The details in this comment are not clear; nevertheless, the reader understands enough that the author of the pesher is warning about the coming devastation of the land by the Roman occupiers.

Similarly, from the same commentary

> "Woe to him who makes his companion drunk, spilling out his venom to intoxicate him so that he may gaze at his festivals" [Hab 2:15]. Its meaning is about the Wicked Priest, who pursued the Teacher of Righteousness to consume him in the heat of his wrath into the abode of his retreat; and at the time set for rest, on the Day of Atonement, he appeared before them to consume them and make them stumble on the Day of Fasting, on the sabbath of their rest. (1QpHab 11:2–8)

Another good example of a commentary is found in the Pesher on Nahum (4QpNah [4Q169]). Nahum prophesied in the late seventh century against the capital of Assyria, Nineveh. He awaited the coming decision, when the Lord would pass judgment on it and its inhabitants. Nahum compared Nineveh to a lion's den, where the young lions would be killed so that they could take no more prey. The author of the Qumran pesher quotes some of the prophecy of Nahum and refers the words to his contemporary situation:

PESHER ON HABAKKUK (1QpHab)

"Where the lion goes, there is the lion's cub, without anyone disturbing him" (Nah 2:11). The meaning of it is about Demetrius, the king of Greece, who sought to enter Jerusalem on the advice of the Seekers after Smooth Things. But he did not enter (it), for God did not allow the city to be handed over to the kings of Greece from the time of Antiochus until the coming of the leaders of the Kittim. But later it will be trampled under their feet.... (4QpNah [4Q169] 3–4 i 1–4)

That "Demetrius" was Demetrios III Eukairos (95–88 B.C.), who was invited to attack Jerusalem by the Pharisees (called here "Seekers after Smooth Things"). "Antiochus" was Antiochus IV Epiphanes (175–164 B.C.), who sought to eliminate Judaism and hellenize the Jewish people.

So much for the commentaries called *pěšārîm*. There are also some documents that are not *pěšārîm* in the strict sense, but use the pesher technique of interpretation: for example, 11QMelch (11Q13), 4QFlor (4Q174), 4QTestim (4Q15), 4QCatena[a] (4Q177). Such documents contain quotations and short explanations of passages taken from various books of the OT.

2. Isolated Quotations of Scripture

Throughout the writings of the Qumran Essenes, especially in their sectarian literature and apart from the *pěšārîm*, quotations of Scripture are introduced to explain a tenet or to illustrate a feature of their belief. They are used often as proof-texts. Such quotations are introduced by formulas that use the verb *'āmar*, "say," or *kātab*, "write."

(a) With *kātab*, eight formulas are found:

   (i) *kî kēn kātûb*, "for thus it is written" (1QS 5:15; CD 11:18)
   (ii) *ka'ăšer kātûb*, "as it was written" (1QS 8:14; CD 7:19)
   (iii) *ka'ăšer kātûb běsēpher Môšēh*, "as it was written in the book of Moses" (4QFlor 1:2)
   (iv) *kî kātûb*, "for it was written" (CD 11:20)
   (v) *kātûb běsēpher Yěšā'yāh hannābî'*, "what was written in the book of Isaiah the prophet" (4QFlor 1:15)
   (vi) *wěhēmmāh ăšer kātûb 'ălêhem ba'ăharît [hayyāmîm]* "and these are the ones about whom it was written in the end of [days]" (4QCatena^a 1-4:7)
   (vii) *wě'ēn kātûb kî*, "and is it not written that...?" (CD 9:5)
   (viii) *wě'al hannāśî' kātûb*, "and concerning the prince it was written" (CD 5:1)

(b) With *'āmar*, six formulas are found:

   (i) *ka'ăšer 'āmar*, "as it said" (or possibly, "as He said") (CD 7:8 [19:51])
   (ii) *'ăšer 'āmar* "as it/He said" (CD 4:20)
   (iii) *wa'ăšer 'āmar*, "and as for what it/He said" (CD 9:2; 16:6)
   (iv) *'ăšer 'āmar ēl 'ălêhem*, "about whom God said" (CD 6:13; 8:9)
   (v) *'ăšer 'āmar Yěša'yāh*, "what Isaiah said" (CD 6:7–8)

(vi) *kî hû' 'ăšer 'āmar,* "for that is what it/He said"
(CD 10:16; 16:15).

Many of these introductory formulas find their Greek counterparts in NT formulas, for example, *kathōs gegraptai,* "as it was
written" (Luke 2:23; Acts 15:15); *kathōs eirēken,* "as He said" (Heb
4:3). Moreover, these Qumran introductory formulas are closer to
the NT formulas than are the Mishnaic formulas that use the same
verbs.[1]

The isolated quotations of the OT in the Qumran writings
are of different types. Some of them are quoted in the literal or
historical sense; that is, the quotation is exact, and the original
author's intention is retained (CD 10:16–17, citing Deut 5:12,
"Observe the Sabbath, to keep it holy"). Other quotations mod-
ernize the meaning; that is, they make it refer in the same sense to
a contemporary person or event (CD 1:13–14, citing Hos 4:16 and
applying it to the Qumran sect). Still others accommodate the biblical text; that is, they wrest it from its context and give it a different meaning (1QS 8:13–16, citing Isa 40:3, "In the desert, prepare
the way of the LORD," applying it to the desert retreat of the
Essenes). Again, other quotations are eschatological; that is, adapt-
ing an OT eschatological passage to the Essene end-time (1QM
10:1–2, citing Deut 7:21–22, "the Lord, your God, will clear these
nations away before you").

3. Principles of Interpretation

In most instances, the Essene interpretation of Scripture
assumes the form of literal exegesis, which is unlike that of Philo
and other Alexandrian interpreters, whose interpretation is often
allegorical, figurative, or symbolic. The Essene interpretation was
known as "the exact interpretation of the Law" (*pĕrûš hattôrāh,* CD
4:8) and "the study of the Law" (*midraš hattôrāh*). The passage in the
Manual of Discipline that explains why the Essenes were in their
desert retreat says, "When these have become a community in
Israel…and walk to the desert to open there His path, as it stands
written, 'In the desert prepare the way of ••••, make straight a

path for our God' (Isa 40:3). This is the study of the Law, which He ordered through Moses" (1QS 8:12–15). The Essenes considered such study a way of discerning the will of God: what God had hidden from Israel of old, but was discovered by "the Interpreter of the Law" (*dôrēš hattôrāh*, 1QS 8:11–12), who may have been the Teacher of Righteousness:

> God told Habakkuk to write what was going to happen to the last generation, but He did not inform him about the consummation of the age. And as for what it says, "So that the one who reads it may run," its meaning is about the Teacher of Righteousness, to whom God has made known all the mysteries of the words of His servants, the Prophets. (1QpHab 7:1–4)

As a result, the Essenes became "the men of truth, those who observe the Law, whose hands do not desert the service of the truth" (1QpHab 7:10–12).

There are some instances, however, of allegorical interpretation, for example, in CD 4:13–18: "'Panic, pit, and net against you, O dweller of the earth' (Isa 24:17). The meaning of it is (this): they are the three nets of Belial, of which Levi, son of Jacob, spoke, in which he traps Israel. The first is fornication; the second, wealth; and the third, defilement of the Temple...." Even though the Essenes insisted on "the exact interpretation of the Law," that did not prevent them from giving words a figurative meaning at times, especially by transposing letters in a word, exploiting textual variants, and separating words in atomistic fashion. Such figurative meanings are found in the Essene *pěšārîm*.

4. Parabiblical Writings

Parabiblical writings are called sometimes the "rewritten Bible," because they take a biblical narrative and recast it with embellishments or descriptions not found in the original story. This recasting is not a commentary, but rather an expanded retelling of the biblical narrative. Such writings are also called at times "pseudepigrapha," which means that the author writes his book, not in his own name, but in that of some person of biblical times (e.g., Abraham, Adam, Elijah).

A good example of a new parabiblical writing is found in the Aramaic Genesis Apocryphon of Qumran Cave 1 (1Qap Gen). The title that the original editor put on it is really a misnomer; a better title for it would have been "The Book of the Ancestors," because it rewrites the biblical story of Lamech and Noah, Abram and Sarai. Resembling the *Book of Jubilees* in its rewriting, it tells of the birth of Noah, a wondrous child, whom Lamech

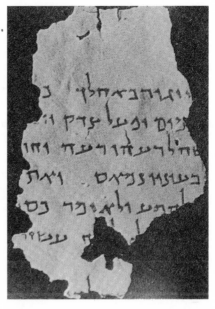

FRAGMENTS OF PSALMS 15 AND 16 FROM THE CAVE OF THE LETTER IN NAḤAL ḤEVER

suspects was conceived by Bit-enosh, his mother, consorting with one of the Nephilim (fallen angels). It also continues with the story of Noah and the deluge and the division of the earth after the deluge among the descendants of Noah. It also recounts the biblical story of Abram to the end of Genesis 14, and a little beyond, but not up to Gen 15:6, where one would love to know how that important verse ("He [Abram] believed the LORD; and He reckoned it to him as righteousness") was rendered in Aramaic.

Some of the embellishments are a description of Sarai's beauty (20:1–8); a plague on Pharaoh and his household (20:9–30); Abram's vision of God (21:8–10); his journey through the promised land (21:10–20); the laying on of hands to cure the Pharaoh (20:22). In 21:23—22:26, the Aramaic text is almost a literal translation of the Hebrew words of Genesis 14.

In this category of pseudepigrapha or parabiblical texts, one has to include the *Book of Enoch*. In the genealogy in Gen 5:18–24, Enoch is listed as the son of Jared, who lived in close relation to

God for 365 years: "and he was not, for God took him"; that is, he was carried up to God's presence, and no one could find his burial site.[2] The transfer of Enoch developed into many legends in pre-Christian Judaism; the most important of them is *1 Enoch*, known for a long time in Ethiopic. Now, however, it has come to light in its Aramaic original in many Qumran fragments (e.g., 1QEnGiants^{a-b} [1Q23–24], 2QEnGiants [2Q26], 4QEn^{a-g} [4Q201–202, 204, 207], 4QEnastr^{a-d} [4Q208–211], 4QEnGiants^{a-e} [4Q203, 4Q530–533]). These documents not only have the original language of *1 Enoch* but include the story of Enoch Giants, which was unknown before the discovery of the Qumran Scrolls.

In the Ethiopic (pre-Qumran) form, *1 Enoch* has the following five parts: (a) Book of Watchers (chaps. 1—36); (b) Book of Parables/Similitudes (chaps. 37—71); (c) Book of Luminaries (Astronomical Book, chaps. 72—82); (d) Book of Dreams (Animal Apocalypse, chaps. 82—90); (e) Epistle of Enoch (chaps. 91—108). Part of *1 Enoch* exists also in a Greek translation.

The Qumran form of Enoch, all in Aramaic, also has five parts, but not the same as the Ethiopic form, nor in the same order: (a) Book of Luminaries (Astronomical Book, in a much extended text); (b) Book of Watchers; (c) Book of Giants (which did not exist in the Ethiopic form and is new); (d) Book of Dreams (Animal Apocalypse); (e) Epistle of Enoch. Noteworthy in this Qumran form of Enoch is the absence of the Book of Parables/Similitudes (= *1 Enoch* 37—71), in which a mysterious figure appears called diversely "son of man," "messiah," "chosen one," and "righteous one." The multiple predication of such titles of one figure is an important precedent for the multiple predication of titles of Jesus of Nazareth in the NT. The editor of these Enoch texts, J. T. Milik, claimed that the Parables were a later (Christian) composition, which was substituted for the Book of Giants, because the latter was so popular among the Manichaeans. Very few scholars have followed Milik in this view, insisting rather that the Book of Giants was composed also in pre-Christian times, perhaps by others than the Essenes.

There is also the *Book of Jubilees*, which is a rewritten Hebrew form of the narratives in Genesis and the first part of Exodus (up to about chap. 19). It purports to be a divine revelation to Moses, who is summoned to Mount Sinai to learn about the future apostasy of Israel and its restoration. This message is dictated to Moses by an angel of the Presence, who reads from heavenly tablets, which are quoted in chaps. 2—50. The author rewrites the biblical stories to communicate his own theological interpretations. The book is named "Jubilees," because it divides the history of the world into 50 periods of 49 years each—a jubilee = 49 years. Fifteen fragmentary copies of this writing have been found in various Qumran caves (e.g., 1Q17–18; 2Q19–20; 3Q5; 4Q216–224; 11Q12).

Another important example of the rewriting of OT books is the Temple Scroll (11QTemple^a [11Q19]),[3] which emphasizes the role of the Mosaic Law in the life of the Essene community. After the mention of the covenant made with Israel on Mount Sinai, the text presents regulations about the construction of the Temple (cols. 3–13), about festivals to be celebrated and sacrifices to be offered in the Temple (cols. 13–29), about the courts of the Temple (cols. 30–45), and what may not be brought into the Temple (cols. 45–47). The last columns (48–65) contain a collection of regulations, mostly drawn from biblical Deuteronomy. The regulations are presented in this document as instructions coming from the lips of God; wherever the biblical text reads, "and the LORD said…," this document changes the third person to the first person.

Also important as an example of the rewritten Bible is "Some Works of the Law" (*miqṣat ma'áśê hattôrāh*) 4QMMT (4Q394–399),[4] which is called a "Halakhic Letter," since it ends with a letter that the Essenes sent to Jewish authorities in Jerusalem, giving an account of the way they interpret the Law and inviting their opponents to amend their lives and agree with the interpretation of the writers. The letter seems to have begun with a discussion of the 364-day solar calendar that the Essenes followed (part of the beginning is lost). Then follow 22 legal items, on which the Essenes differ from the Jerusalemites: "Remember David, who was a man among the pious, and he was freed of many afflictions and was forgiven. We have also written to you some of the works of the Law, which we believe are good for you and for your people, for we recognize that you have intelligence and knowledge of the Law.…It shall be reckoned for you as righteousness, when you do what is upright and good before Him" (4Q398 14–17 ii 1–7).

5. Son of God Text

A remarkable document coming from Qumran Cave 4 is 4Q246, which is called often "the Son of God text." It shows how Palestinian Jews were interpreting OT phrases and ideas to suit a sectarian tenet. The text is an apocalyptic writing, a column and a half of nine lines each, which tells of a person who falls down before a king and predicts that the king will have a son who is to be great. The text is fragmentary; its first column lacks the last half of each of the nine lines. So it is not possible to say who the subject of the prediction is. The king's "son" is actually an editor's restoration of 1:7, but it is not restored with certainty; in any case, the subject is someone different from the king. Line 1:7 reads thus: "[Your son] shall also be great upon the earth" (*[’aph bĕrāk] rab lihwēh ‘al ’ar‘ā’*) and lines 1:9—2:1 continue with: "He shall be called [son of] the [gr]eat [God], and by His name shall he be named; he shall be hailed son of God, and they shall call him son of the Most High" (*[hû’ bar ’Ēl r]abbā’ yitqĕrē’ ’ûbišmēh yitkannēh / bĕrēh dî ’Ēl yit’āmar ûbar ‘elyôn yiqrôneh*) and in 2:5, "his kingdom shall be an everlasting kingdom" (*malkûtēh malkût ‘ôlām*).

This text is important, not only because it includes phrases from the OT, but also because echoes of it are found in the NT. In the OT, one reads at times of "sons of God" (e.g., Gen 6:2, 4; Job 1:6; 2:1) or "sons of the Most High" (Ps 82:6) in the plural. The singular "son of God" is the title given to an angel in Dan 3:25 (in Aramaic), or (in a collective sense) to Israel in Wis 18:13 (in Greek), or to a righteous person in Wis 2:18 (again in Greek); but the singular expression, "son of God," is not found in Hebrew either in the OT or the Qumran Scrolls. Moreover, echoes of this Son of God text are sounded in the NT, especially in the infancy narrative of the Lucan Gospel. There the angel Gabriel addresses Mary and announces that the child to be born of her "shall be great" (Luke 1:32 [compare 4Q246 1:7]); "shall be hailed Son of the Most High" (1:32 [cf. 4Q246 2:1]); "shall be called Son of God" (1:35 [cf. 4Q246 2:1); and "of his kingdom there shall be no end" (1:33 [cf. 4Q246 2:5]). Is this similarity coincidental? Or is Luke "dependent in some way, directly or indirectly, on this long-lost text from Qumran," as J. J. Collins has asked.[5] The title is found in other NT writings: Rom 1:4; 2 Cor 1:19.

VII

APOCRYPHAL, SAPIENTIAL, LITURGICAL, AND ESCHATOLOGICAL LITERATURE

In addition to the deuterocanonical and parabiblical literature, there are other Qumran texts that were developed independently of the Scriptures, even though some of them quote phrases and verses from the Scriptures: apocryphal, sapiential, liturgical, and eschatological writings.

1. Apocryphal Writings

This genre of literature is not defined easily, and no one knows when the title for it was first developed. "Apocryphal Books" (*apokrypha biblia*) is said to have designated at first "hidden books," that is, books stored away, often because they were composed by pagans or heretics and were not to be read by Christians or Jews. In the Jewish tradition, such books were called *ḥîṣônîm*, "outside" books, and "whoever reads the outside books would have no share in the life to come" (Palestinian Talmud, *Sanhedrin* 10:1). Later on, the title came to mean simply those books that were not canonical, that is, not part of the Jewish or Christian canon.

The writings that are called "deuterocanonical" for Catholic and Eastern Orthodox Christians are included among the "Apocrypha" for Protestant Christians. I have already dealt with the deuterocanonical writings in chapter V, "The Scriptures in the Scrolls," because they are part of the OT. Fragments of such writings have been discovered in Qumran caves—the Epistle of Jeremy, Sirach, and Tobit.

As for the rest of what modern readers call the "Apocrypha," there is hardly a text from among them that has been found in Qumran caves, apart from a tiny fragment of the work often called "Daniel and Suzanna" (4QDanSuz [4Q551]), which is identified only doubtfully as such.

Writings that are similar to the Apocrypha are called "Pseudepigrapha," meaning "falsely attributed books," but there is no standard collection of them. "OT Pseudepigrapha" denotes books attributed to OT figures such as Abraham, Adam, Enoch, Moses. Such writings would include *1 Enoch*, *Book of Jubilees*, and so on, which I have discussed elsewhere under other more adequate headings.

2. Sapiential Writings

Wisdom literature is found in the OT in Job, Proverbs, Qoheleth, Sirach, and the Wisdom of Solomon. The Qumran fragments of such OT texts have been discussed in chapter V, "The Scriptures in the Scrolls." Here I include the noncanonical sapiential texts retrieved from the Qumran caves.

The literary form of the wisdom texts is an *instruction* that often addresses a group or an individual, using imperatives and prohibitions, and giving reasons for good behavior and wise conduct. Among the Qumran fragmentary texts, the most extensive copy is 4QInstruction (4Q415–4Q418a); its Hebrew title is *Mûsār lĕMēwîn*, "Instruction for the Maven/Student."[1] Related to it is 1QInstruction (1Q26). The Instruction begins with a reminder that God will execute judgment on all who do evil and bring all wickedness to an end. Then a senior sage instructs the maven about the use of money, possessions, social relations, and family affairs.

Other examples of sapiential writing are found:

(a) 4QWisText (4Q185), in which a sage instructs "the sons of man" how to become wise, and "simpletons" that they should remember "the miracles that God performed in Egypt, His portents in the land of Ham" (4Q185 1–2 i 9, 14–15).

(b) 4QWiles (4Q184), which describes a lady and all her devices as she tries to seduce the righteous from the path of uprightness: "She is the ruination of all who inherit her, the calamity of all who take hold of her....Her paths are the paths of death" (4Q184 1:8–9).

(c) 4QInstrCompB (4Q424) is an instruction for a student on the dangers of dealing with hypocrites, lazy people, and simpletons. One should rather depend on a prudent man, "an upright man who takes pleasure in judgment and will prosecute those who shift boundaries" (4Q424 3:79).

(d) 4QBeat (4Q525) is a collection of beatitudes, similar to those in Sir 14:20 and Matt 5:3–10. Their theological orientation, however, is different, for they are sapiential in tone, not eschatological.

(e) There are also several hymns that contain wisdom elements (e.g., 11QHymns^{a-b} [11Q15–26]; David's Compositions in 11QPs^a [11Q5] 27:22–23).

Many of these wisdom writings depict Wisdom as a woman (e.g., Sir 51:13–20 in 11QPs^a [11Q5] 21; Hymn to the Creator in 11QPs^a [11Q5] 26), and Folly as a lady (in 4QWiles [4Q184]). The main reason for such a depiction is the feminine gender of the noun *ḥokmāh*, "wisdom."

3. Liturgical Writings

Apart from the biblical writings, a number of fragments from the Qumran caves reveal the way the Essenes prayed and worshiped God, not only on feast days but also on Sabbaths, which they strove to keep holy.

(a) *Feast Days.* Together with the rest of the Jews in Judea, the Essenes celebrated the feasts listed in their Hebrew Scriptures. In addition to the weekly Sabbath, these feasts were (i) Passover (*pesaḥ*) on 14 Nisan, the first month (Exod 12:1–14); (ii) Unleavened Bread (*maṣṣôt*) on 15–21 Nisan (Exod 12:15–20); (iii) Weeks or the feast of Harvest (*ḥaqqāṣîr*) on 15 Sivan, the third month (Exod 23:16a); (iv) Day of Atonement (*yôm hakkippurîm*) on 10 Tishri, the seventh month (Exod 30:10); (v) Booths or Ingathering (*hā'āsip*) on 15–22 Tishri, the seventh month (Exod 23:16b).

In addition to these feasts celebrated in common with other Jews, the Essenes recognized other days as festive. Besides the Feast of Weeks or Pentecost, when the harvest of New Grain (*minḥāh ḥădāšāh*) was offered to Yahweh (11QTemple[a] [11Q19] 18:10–13), there was also (i) the Pentecost of New Wine (*yayin ḥādāš*) on 3 Sivan, the third month: "You will count for yourselves from the day you bring the new meal-offering to Yahweh, the bread as the first-fruits, seven weeks, seven Sabbaths complete they will be until the morrow of the seventh Sabbath; you will count fifty days, and will bring new wine for a libation..." (11QTemple[a] [11Q19] 19:11–14); (ii) the Pentecost of New Oil (*šemen ḥādāš*) on 22 Elul, the sixth month: "You will count for yourselves from this day seven weeks, seven times (seven), forty-nine days, seven Sabbaths complete; you will count fifty days, and you will offer new oil from the dwelling-places of the tribes of Israelites, a half *hin* from each tribe, new oil crushed [   ] fresh oil upon the altar of holocaust as fresh-fruits before Yahweh" (11QTemple[a] [11Q19] 21:12–16); (iii) the Feast of Wood (*ḥāg hā'ēṣîm*) on 23–30(?) Elul, the sixth month: "They shall offer on the feast of Wood a burnt-offering for Yahweh" (11QTemple[a] [11Q19] 23:3; see also 43:4; 11QTemple [11Q20] 6:12, 15–16); (iv) the Day of Waving the Sheaf (*yôm hănîpat hā'ômer*) on 26 Nisan, the first month (11QTemple[a] [11Q19] 18:10), a text too poorly preserved to quote further.

It is not known whether the Essenes celebrated the feasts of "Dedication" (*ḥannûkāh*) or "Lots" (*pûrîm*). These names do not occur in the Qumran writings.

(b) The most extensive liturgical text is the *Hôdāyôt*, "Thanksgiving Psalms," which was retrieved from Caves 1 and 4 (1QH [1Q35], 4QH [4Q427–431], 4QpapH [4Q432], and perhaps 4Q433, 433a). They are called Thanksgiving Psalms, because a number of them begin with *'ôdēkāh*, "I thank You (Lord), because...." Many interpreters of these psalms think that the first person singular refers to the Teacher of Righteousness, who is praising God for His help in the role that he is playing in the community and in the time of his persecution: for example,

70

> I thank You, Lord, because You have enlightened my face
> with Your covenant, but they [my opponents] are authors
> of lies and seers of deceit; they have concocted against
> me a devilish plot...to change Your Law, which You have
> inscribed on my heart, with flattering things (that they
> announce) to Your people. They have withheld from the
> thirsty the drink of knowledge and given them vinegar to
> drink. (1QH^a 12 [old 4]:5, 9–12)

Other thanksgiving psalms express the sentiments of members of
the Essene community, as they worship the Creator and praise Him
for the gifts they have received from His bounty. These psalms
echo many phrases of the canonical Psalter, but only rarely do they
imitate the parallelism of clauses found in that Psalter.

   (c) Another lengthy liturgical text is the "Songs for the
Sabbath Sacrifice," which has been found in Caves 4 and 11 and
also at Masada (4QShirShabb^{a-h} [4Q400–407]; 11QShirShabb
[11Q17]; MasShirShabb [Mas1k]). This text has hymns for thirteen
Sabbaths, that is, one each for a quarter of the 52-week, 364-day
calendar year. The individual Sabbaths are dated, for example,
"Hymn of the holocaust for the sixth Sabbath on the ninth (day) of
the second month" (MasShirShabb 1:8). The hymns recall the
wondrous deeds of the Creator God, His knowledge and His reve-
lations, and summon the Essenes to adore and thank Him.

   (d) Still other shorter texts can be mentioned here, such as
"Blessings" (4QBer^{a-d} [4Q286–289]), the "Psalms of Joshua"
(4QapJosh^{a-b} [4Q378–379]); noncanonical Psalms (4QNoncan-
PsA-B [4Q380–381]); Psalms that begin, "Bless the Lord, O my
soul" (4QBarNaf^{a-e} [4Q434–438]), with the beginning borrowed
from canonical Psalms 103–4.

   (e) 4QprNab ar (4Q242), "the Prayer of Nabonidus," is an
important text related to the Book of Daniel, chap. 4. It consists of
eight fragmentary lines of Aramaic and reads as follows:

> The words of the prayer which Nabonidus, king of
> Babylon, the great king, uttered when he was struck with
> an evil ulcer by God's decree in Teima. I, Nabonidus, was
> struck with an evil ulcer for seven years; but because God

set His face on me, He cured me. As for my sin, He remitted it. An exorcist (he was a Jew from the exiles) came to me, saying, "Make known and write it down: to grant honor and glory to the name of God Most High." So then I wrote, "I was struck with a bad ulcer in Teima by the decree of God Most High. For seven years I prayed to the gods of silver and gold, of bronze and iron, of wood, stone, and clay, because I thought they were gods." (1:1–8)

Nabonidus was the last king (556–539 B.C.) of the Neo-Babylonian dynasty, who spent seven years in the oasis of Teima (a site in modern Saudi Arabia). The author of the Book of Daniel adopted this story about Nabonidus in chap. 4 and changed the name of the king to that of the great persecutor of Israel, Nebuchadnezzar, and Teima was replaced by Babylon, whence he came. The exorcist in the Nabonidus story became rather Daniel, who urged Nebuchadnezzar to pray (Dan 4:27).

(f) 11QPs^a [11Q5] 27:5–8 tells of David's Compositions, among which were "hymns to be sung before the altar over the continuous holocaust of each day, for all the days of the year, 364; for the Sabbath offerings, 52 hymns; for the offerings of the first days of the months and all the feast-days, and for the Day of Atonement, 30 hymns...."

4. Eschatological Writings

Many Qumran texts speak of the end-time, using phrases like "in the final days" (*bĕ'aḥārît hayyāmîm*, 1QSa 1:1), "the final age" (*haqqēṣ hā'aḥărôn*, 1QpHab 7:7), or "at the end-time of wrath" (*bĕqēṣ ḥārôn*, CD 1:5). The reason for this emphasis is that the Essenes believed that they were already living in that last age. Some of these phrases are found in the Pesharim and the Parabiblical Writings that have already been discussed (*1 Enoch*, Rule of the Congregation [1QSa], etc.), which have eschatological passages.

(a) The most important eschatological writing among the Qumran scrolls is the War Scroll, called in Hebrew, *Serek ham-*

milḥāmāh (1QM [1Q33]), one of the seven scrolls found in Cave 1.[2] The upper 15 lines of the 19 columns of this text are fairly well preserved; and fragments of six more copies of the text were found in Cave 4 (4QM^a-f [4Q491–96]). The text of 1QM is written in Herodian script and dated roughly to the end of the first century B.C. Yigael Yadin, who was a general in the Israeli army during the First Arab–Jewish War, wrote an important commentary on 1QM.[3] In it, he showed that the writing was composed in the second half of the first century B.C., arguing from the details of troop formation and the armor described. He believed that the author had made use of Roman military treatises such as *De re militari* in his composition.

The War Scroll is a book of instructions for the eschatological war that the sons of light (the Qumran community) are going to wage against the sons of darkness (the Kittim [Roman occupiers of Judea] and other opponents of the community, such as Moabites, Edomites, Philistines). They believed that the war would last for 40 years, during which God would come down with His angels to do battle along with the sons of light against their enemies. Columns of 1QM describe the army, its formation, battle array, and equipment (trumpets, banners). Other columns describe the role of priests and levites in the battle: their prayers, exhortations, hymns, and slogans. Although it is said that the war would last for 40 years, it specifies that there would be six-year campaigns, for there was to be no war in the seventh or sabbatical years. The motivation for the war is based on Dan 11:30, 32: "those who forsake the holy covenant...who violate the covenant."

(b) Another eschatological writing found in the Qumran caves is the "New Jerusalem," seven copies of which come from Caves 1, 2, 4, 5, 11 (1QNJ ar [1Q32]; 2QNJ ar [2Q24]; 4QNJ^a-c ar [4Q554, 554a, 555]; 5QNJ ar [5Q15]; 11QNJ ar [11Q18]). This writing describes how the Jerusalem of the end-time is to be built. It mentions a guide who leads a seer about the new city and shows him the streets, blocks, gates, towers, and staircases, along with the dimensions of each.

VIII

BELIEFS AND PRACTICES OF THE SECT:
Dualism, Eschatology, Messianism, Calendar

In the eschatological writings that were discussed toward the end of the preceding chapter, it was found that the Essenes of Qumran believed that they were already living in the end-time. Such a belief not only called for a mode of conduct or behavior that was appropriate to it but also set them apart from other contemporary Jews such as the Pharisees and the Sadducees. The life and conduct of the Essenes relied very much on the data of the Scriptures, which they interpreted exactly and strictly, but they were governed also by their eschatological convictions.

On the one hand, the belief of the Essenes did not differ from the teachings of other Jews, in that they too affirmed monotheism and the observance of the Mosaic Law and the writings of the Prophets. The Essenes likewise uttered, "Hear, O Israel, Yahweh, is our God, Yahweh alone" (Deut 6:4), and pledged "to seek God with all one's heart and with all one's soul and to do what is good and upright before Him, as He ordered through Moses and all His servants, the Prophets" (1QS 1:1–3). So they expressed their reverence and respect for "the God of Israel" (1QS 3:24), the God of their ancestors. In the Psalms Scroll of Qumran Cave 11, which was like a prayer book of the community, the Essenes sang to God with many of the psalms of the canonical psalter. Yet it contains also a "Hymn to the Creator" and uses phrases from Jer 10:12–13 and Ps 135:7:

Great and holy is Yahweh, the holiest in every generation. Majesty goes before Him, and the swarm of many
waters follows Him. Grace and fidelity attend His presence; fidelity, justice, and righteousness are the founda-
tion of His throne. He has separated light from deep
darkness; He has established the dawn with the knowledge of His heart. Then all the angels beheld it and sang
aloud, for He has made them see what they did not
know. He crowns mountains with fruit, good food for
every living being. Blessed be He who makes the earth
by His power, who established the world by His wisdom!
By His understanding He has stretched out the heavens
and caused the wind to go forth from its storehouses. He
has made the lightning for the rain and caused mists to
rise from the end of the earth. (11QPs[a] 26:9–15)

In a special way, the Essenes manifested their reverence for
the God whom they served by the way they wrote His name. Usually,
they used the archaic name *'Ēl*, which literally means "Mighty
One" (1QS 1:2, 7, 8; CD 1:2, 10), writing it even in paleo-Hebrew
script to enhance its dignity (4QAgesCreat [4Q180] 1:1; 4Q183 l ii
3; 1QpMic [1Q14] 12:3). Sometimes they join it with various epi-
thets: *'Ēl 'elyôn*, "God Most High" (1QH[a] 12 [old 4]:31) or *'Ēl
'ēlîm*, "God of gods" (1QM 14:16); *'Ēl haddē'ôt*, "God of knowledge" (1QS 3:15; 1QH[a] 9 [old 1]:26); etc. The usual OT name
'Elôhîm is used, but less frequently (1QS 8:14; 1QM 10:4, 7), but
also in the form *'Elôhê ṣēbā'ôt*, "God of the Hosts" (1QSb [1Q28b]
4:25). *'Elôhîm* is substituted at times for *YHWH* in OT quotations
(1QM 10:7, quoting Num 10:9). Another substitute is *Šadday*, "the
Almighty" (4QTestim [4Q175] 1:11, as in Num 24:16). In the
Thanksgiving Psalms, the name *'Ădônāy*, "Lord," appears very frequently (1QH[a] 10 [old 2]:20, 31; 3:19, 37; etc.).

The tetragrammaton *YHWH*, which is called "the name of
the Glorified One" (1QS 6:27), occurs more frequently than one
might expect (e.g., 4Q158 1–2:16, 18; 4:8; 7–8:3; 4QFlor [4Q174]
1–2 i 3; 21:1; 11QTemple[a] 21:3, 8, 10); and occasionally four dots
(••••) are substituted for it: 1QIsa[a] 33:7 (= Isa 40:7); 4QSam[c]
(4Q53) 1:3; 4QTestim (4Q175) 1:19. In 4QLXXLev[b] gr (4Q120),

the tetragrammaton is written in Greek as *IAŌ*, the way that it is found in Greek writers of the patristic period.

These different ways of writing the name of God not only reveal the reverence the Essenes had for the Creator, but also show the way they tended to avoid pronouncing His sacred name as *Yahweh*. The common vocalization of the four consonants is known from Origen's *Hexapla*, where he transcribed the pronunciation of the Hebrew in Greek as *IABЄ* The tetragrammaton, written in Hebrew characters, was employed even in Greek translations of OT books, when those translations were made by Jewish scribes. Christian scribes, however, translated the tetragrammaton in the Septuagint as *ho Kyrios*, "the Lord," and that became the common practice for centuries.

On the other hand, the Essenes differed in their insistence on a dualistic division of human beings, on a conviction about the end-time, and on a teaching about the coming of an anointed agent of salvation for God's people.

1. Dualism

The Essenes believed that God, in creating human beings, divided them into two classes that would be governed by two different spirits. This belief is enunciated mainly in their rule book, the Manual of Discipline:

> ...that they may live perfectly before Him in accordance with all that has been revealed about their appointed times; to love all the sons of light, each according to his lot in God's plan, and to hate all the sons of darkness, each according to his guilt in God's vindication. (1QS 1:8–11)

The "sons of light" were the members of the Essene community, and the "sons of darkness" were the rest of the Jews of Judea and others who disagreed with them and refused to join them.

> He created human beings to rule the world and placed within them two spirits so that they would walk accord-

ing to them until the time of His visitation: they are the spirits of fidelity and iniquity. From the spring of light come the generations of fidelity, and from the spring of darkness come the generations of iniquity. In the hand of the Prince of Lights is the governance of all the sons of righteousness; they walk on paths of light. But in the hand of the Angel of Darkness is the complete domination of all the sons of iniquity; they walk on paths of darkness. From the Angel of Darkness comes also the corruption of all the sons of righteousness; and all their sins, their wicked deeds, their guilt, and their transgressions are under its governance in accordance with God's mysteries....However, the God of Israel and His angel of fidelity assist all the sons of light. For He created the spirits of light and darkness, and on them He established every deed; on their paths He based every action. He loves the one everlastingly and always takes pleasure in its acts; but the other He abominates and forever hates its ways. (1QS 3:17—4:1)

The rule book also spells out in detail the effects that these spirits have on those who are dominated by them:

These are their paths in the world:...to establish in the human heart respect for God's precepts. It is a spirit of meekness, patience, generous compassion, everlasting goodness, intelligence, mighty wisdom that trusts all the deeds of God and depends on His abundant mercy.... These are the counsel of the spirit for the sons of fidelity in this world. As for the visitation of all who walk in this spirit, it will be healing, great peace in a long life, fruitfulness, together with every blessing and eternal joy.... But to the spirit of iniquity belong greed, sloth in the service of justice, wickedness, deceit, pride, haughtiness of heart, dishonesty, trickery, cruelty, impudence, lust..., so that man walks on all the paths of darkness and guile....As for the visitation of all who walk in this spirit, it will be an abundance of afflictions at the hands of all

77

the angels of destruction, eternal damnation by the searing wrath of God.... (1QS 4:2–13)

The background of this view of humanity can be found in the mythical account in Gen 6:1–5, where "the sons of God" (i.e., angels) took as wives "the daughters of men," to whom children were born that became "the Nephilim" (i.e., the Fallen Ones [= Fallen Angels]), and God "saw that the wickedness of man was great upon the earth." So the Essenes explained the problem of evil: Spirits of Good and Evil are struggling with each other for domination over the present world, and even in the hearts of human beings. The spirit of Evil is known by various names: "Spirit of Iniquity," "Angel of Darkness," "Belial," "Satan," or "Mastemah."

This dualism is often called "cosmic dualism," but it is not extended to all physical pairs (like day/night, sun/moon, light/darkness, male/female), as in some other myths. It is mainly an "ethical dualism," restricted to the conduct of human beings. It is also a doctrine about human conduct as controlled by Jewish monotheism. For the Creator God is the one who puts the two spirits in human beings and who will judge their conduct at the time of His visitation.

2. Eschatology

The Essenes were convinced that they had begun to live in what they regarded as the end-time. It still had a future for them, for they looked forward to its consummation in a war at the end of time, when God and His angels would come down to do battle along with the sons of light against the sons of darkness, as we have seen already in the discussion of the War Scroll (1QM and 4QM). So life was not only a struggle between good and evil, dominated by the two spirits already received from the Creator God, but also a battle with its climax in that war of the end-time.

The Essenes also believed that the world would end in a universal conflagration:

...then the torrents of Belial will overflow all the high banks like a devouring fire in all their water-canals, destroying every tree, green or dry....It will consume the foundations of clay and the tract of dry land; it will burn the bases of mountains and turn the roots of flint rock into streams of lava. It will consume right up to the Great Deep, and the torrents of Belial will break into Abaddon....The earth will cry out at the calamity that overtakes the world, and all its schemers will scream, and all who are on it will go crazy and melt away in the great calamity.... (1QH^a 11 [old 3]:29–34)

The Essenes also thought that a new world would be born from such a conflagration, a new world that they describe figuratively, using personification and images drawn from childbirth and a boat tossed on waves of a sea: "They have set my soul like a boat in the depths of the sea, like a fortified city opposite its enemies. I was in distress like a woman giving birth the first time, when her labor-pains come upon her and distress racks the mouth of her womb to begin the birth in the 'crucible' of the pregnant woman" (1QH^a 11 [old 3]:6–8). This eschatological belief was governed also by a conviction that the Creator God had determined in advance all that would happen to His creation:

From the God of knowledge comes all there is and all there will be. Before they existed, He established their entire design. When they have come into being, at their appointed time, they carry out all their tasks according to His glorious design, without changing anything. In His hand are the laws of all things, and He supports them all in all their tasks. (1QS 3:15–17)

This predeterminism was applied also to human beings, as we have seen already in the dualistic division of humanity and the Essene attempt to explain the problem of evil. Unfortunately, we never learn how the Essenes put the two convictions together in a logical way. This Essene conviction was noted even by Josephus, who compared it to that of the Pharisees and the Sadducees. He called it "Fate" (*heimarmenē*) and thought of it as a goddess; he recorded:

> The Pharisees maintain that certain events are the work of Fate, but not all; some depend on ourselves, whether they will occur. The group of the Essenes, however, declares that Fate is the mistress of everything, and that nothing happens to humans unless it is according to her decree. But the Sadducees do away with Fate, claiming that there is no such thing...and that all things happen through our own power. (*Ant.* 13.5.9 §§172–73)

3. Messianism

Part of the eschatological belief of the Essenes was a conviction that near the end of human history God would send anointed agents to bring about the final salvation of His people.

The discussion of this topic, however, is complicated, because many students of the QL fail to restrict the meaning of the word *māšîaḥ*, "anointed one" or "messiah," to a figure who properly is so named. For instance, it is used often of the "Servant of Yahweh" in Isaiah, in a book where *māšîaḥ* occurs only once, and then only of Cyrus, the king of Persia, who was not a Jew (Isa 45:1); it is never predicated of the Servant in that biblical writing. The word *māšîaḥ* occurs 39 times in the Hebrew OT, but never in the Pentateuch (Genesis to Deuteronomy). In the vast majority of the occurrences, it designates a historical king of the Davidic dynasty governing at a given time. The only time that it appears in the sense of an awaited or coming anointed one is Dan 9:25–26, "until the coming of an anointed one, a prince" (*'ad māšîaḥ nāgîd*) there shall be seven weeks....After sixty-two weeks, an anointed one shall be cut down...."[1]

There are many passages in QL where the Essene form of messianism is presented. The most important passage is found in the rule book, the Manual of Discipline; it reads: "...they shall be governed by the first regulations, by which the men of the Community began to be instructed, until the coming of a prophet and the Messiahs of Aaron and Israel" (*'ad bô' nābî' ûmĕšîḥê 'ahărôn wĕyiśrā'ēl*, 1QS 9:11). Here the expectation includes a prophet (i.e., the prophet like Moses mentioned in Deut 18:15, 18), a (priestly) *Messiah of Aaron* and a (kingly or Davidic) *Messiah of Israel*. Note the similarity in *'ad māšîaḥ* of Dan 9:25 and *'ad bô'...mĕšîḥê* of 1QS 9:11, both introduced with the same phrase, using *'ad*, "until," which makes it clear that the anointed agent is an awaited being of the future. The Messiah of Aaron does not surprise us, because already in post-monarchical biblical times *māšîaḥ* was used as an adjective and applied in the OT to an "anointed priest," most likely the high priest (Lev 4:3).

Other Qumran texts that speak of two Messiahs are CD 19:35—20:1 ("from the day of the gathering in of the Teacher of the Community until the rising of Messiah from Aaron and from Israel"); 4QD^e (4Q270: "those anointed by the holy Spirit" [mentioned in a context referring to the future]); 4QBer^b (4Q287: "those anointed by His holy Spirit").

Still other Qumran texts speak of one Messiah; the first three to be mentioned here refer to one of the two Messiahs of 1QS 9:11: 1QSa (1Q28a) 2:11–13 ("...when God will beget the Messiah among them," later identified as the "Messiah of Israel"); 1QSa (1Q28a) 2:14–15 ("afterwards the Messiah of Israel will take his seat; then there will sit before him the heads of the thousands of Israel, each according to his dignity"); 1QSa (1Q28a) 2:20–21 ("afterwards the Messiah of Israel will put forth his hands to the food"). In the last two passages, the Messiah of Israel is depicted as subordinate to *hakkôhēn*, "the priest," whom many commentators take to be the Messiah of Aaron, even though he is not so identified explicitly. In CD 12:23—13:1, one reads: "Those who walk according to these [statutes] in the wicked end-time until the rising of the Messiah of Aaron and Israel." Here mention is made of one Messiah coming from both Aaron and Israel. The same expression is found again in CD 14:18–19 ("until the rising of the Messiah of Aaron and Israel") and in CD 19:10–11 ("at the coming of the Messiah of Aaron and Israel"). A clear instance of one Messiah is found in 4QpGen^a (4Q252) 6 (col. 5):3–4 ("until the coming of the righteous Messiah, the Scion of David"); likewise in 4QApocMess (4Q521) 2 ii + 4:1 ("for the heavens and the earth will listen to His Messiah, and all that is in them will not swerve from the commandments…"). The same Messiah is mentioned again in a poorly preserved line (9:3) of the same text. Similarly in pap4QparaKings (4Q382) 16:2 ("[M]essiah of Isr[ael]"). "His Messiah" is restored in 4QFlor (4Q174) 1–2 i 11.

Although only two passages in the OT possibly have *māšîaḥ* as a title for prophets (1 Chr 16:22; Ps 105:15),[2] there are Qumran texts where the word is used clearly of prophets. In four instances it is used with a past-tense verb, so that the meaning "Messiah" cannot be envisaged. Instead, it then means simply "Anointed One(s)." Thus 1QM 11:7–8 ("through Your Anointed Ones, who have perceived Your testimonies, You told us about the times of the battles of Your hands"); 6QD (6Q15) 3:4 ("[they preached rebellion against the commandments of God given] through Moses and also by the holy Anointed Ones…"); CD 2:12 ("He instructed them through [those] anointed with His holy Spirit…"); CD 5:21—6:2 ("they preached rebellion against the commandments of God [given] through Moses and also by His holy Anointed Ones…").

Related to the foregoing four texts is 4QapPent[b] (4Q377) 2 ii 5, where Moses is so entitled: "through the mouth of Moses, His Anointed One." This text is related to the foregoing, because Moses was regarded at times as a prophet (Deut 18:15, 18; 34:10). This brings the summary of messianic belief of the Essenes to a close.

4. Other Sundry Beliefs

Besides the main theological tenets that have been singled out in §§1–3 above, the Essenes cherished various other convictions about angels, the holy Spirit, justification by grace, the New Jerusalem, and astrology.

(a) *Angels.* The main word in Hebrew for "angels" is *mal'ākîm* (lit., "messengers," who bring God's word to human beings); but other names are used too: *qĕdôšîm,* "holy ones," *rûḥôt,* "spirits," *'ēlîm,* "divinities," and even *'ĕlôhîm,* "gods." In Aramaic, one finds *mal'ākîn,* "messengers," *'îrîn,* "watchers," and *qaddîšîn,* "holy ones." Many of the Hebrew titles can be found in a text that is called sometimes "The Angelic Liturgy," or more usually 11QShirShabb (11Q17), cols. 1–5.

Besides the angels mentioned in the OT, Michael, Gabriel, and Raphael (1QM 9:15–16; 4QEn[a] 1 iv 6), the Essenes venerated also Sariel (1QM 9:16) and other angels, whose names are listed in 4QEn[a] 1 iv 1–4: Shemiḥazah, Ḥermoni, Baraq'el, Kokab'el, Ziqi'el, Aratteqoph, Shimsôḥi'el, Sahri'el, Asa'el. Another list of twenty angels is provided in 4QEn[a] 1 iii 5–12.[3] Not all the angels were good, however, since Belial also had his *mal'ākîm*, "angels" (1QM 1:15).

The Essenes believed that they lived in the sight of God's angels and that they were not to expose to the view of these holy creatures any human infirmities or deformities: "No one defiled by human impurities shall enter the assembly…; no one who is defiled in his flesh, paralyzed in his feet or hands, lame, blind, deaf, or dumb…, for the angels of holiness are in their congregation" (1QSa [1Q28a] 2:3–9). Similarly 1QM 7:4–6 ("for the holy angels are together with their armies"); 4QD[a] (4Q266) 8 i 9 ("for the holy angels are in their midst"). The rule book, the Manual of Discipline, describes the goal or destiny of Essene life as a share in the life of the angels: "To those whom God has chosen He has given…an inheritance in the lot of the Holy Ones (*běgôral qědôšîm*). He unites their assembly to the sons of heaven (*běnê šāmayim*)… throughout all future ages" (1QS 11:7–9).

Moreover, the Essenes were convinced that in the great war at the end of time the angels would do battle along with them: "On that day the assembly of the divinities (*'ădat 'ēlîm*) and the congregation of men will confront each other for great destruction" (1QM 1:10); "God's great hand will subdue Belial and all the angels of his dominion and all the men of his lot" (1QM 1:14–15).

(b) *The Holy Spirit.* Borrowing from the OT, especially from the Book of Ezekiel, the idea of "the Spirit of the Lord" (37:1), the Essenes used it often to express their awareness of God's presence among them: "You have spread over me Your holy Spirit so that I may not stumble" (1QH[a] 15 [old 7]:7); "You have delighted me with Your holy Spirit" (1QH[a] 17 [old 9]:32); "I have heeded faithfully Your wondrous secret through Your holy Spirit" (1QH[a] 20 [old 17]:12).

(c) *Justification by Grace*. In the hymn of the community at the end of the Manual of Discipline (1QS 10:1—11:22), the Essenes sing of God's righteousness:

> As for me, I belong to wicked humanity, to the assembly of perverse flesh; my iniquities, my transgressions, my sins together with the wickedness of my heart belong to the assembly doomed to worms and walking in darkness. No human being sets his own path or directs his own steps, for to God alone belongs the judgment of him, and from His hand comes perfection of way....And I, if I stagger, God's grace is my salvation forever. If I stumble because of a sin of the flesh, my judgment is according to the righteousness of God, which stands forever....In His mercy, He has drawn me close (to Him), and with His favors will He render judgment of me. In His righteous fidelity He has judged me; in His bounteous goodness He expiates all my iniquities, and in His righteousness He cleanses me of human defilement and of human sinfulness, that I may praise God for His righteousness and the Most High for His majesty. (1QS 11:9–15)

A similar awareness of God's righteousness is expressed in one of the Thanksgiving Psalms:

> As for me, I know that righteousness does not belong to a human being, nor perfection of way to a son of man. To God Most High belong all the deeds of righteousness, whereas the path of a human being is not set firm....And I said, "It is because of my transgression that I have been abandoned far from Your covenant. But when I recalled Your mighty hand along with the abundance of Your mercy, then I was restored, and I stood up. My spirit strengthened my stance against the blows, because I have based myself on Your graces and on the abundance of Your mercy. For You expiate iniquity to cleanse a human being from guilt by Your righteousness." (1QH^a 12 [old 4]:30–31, 35–38; see also 1QH^a 15 [old 7]:28–30)

In such passages, the Essenes expressed their utter sinfulness and realized that the judgment of them stems from the righteousness of God (*ṣidqat 'Ēl*, 1QS 11:12), His grace (*ḥasdê 'Ēl*, ibid.), and His mercy (*raḥămayw*, 1QS 11:13). The sectarians were convinced that judgment of their lives and conduct lay with God, before whose tribunal they would one day stand and be scrutinized, but also to be acquitted of their guilt by a justifying God.

As a result, the Essenes put much emphasis on being "righteous" (*ṣaddîq*) in God's sight. This is the reason why they referred to their leader as the "Teacher of Righteousness," whom they recognized as an imitator of the righteousness of God. They also made loyalty to this Teacher a matter of supreme importance, as the Pesher on Habakkuk makes clear: "But the righteous one will find life through his fidelity" [Hab 2:4b]. The meaning of it concerns all those observing the Law in the house of Judah, whom God will free from the house of judgment because of their effort and their loyalty to the "Teacher of Righteousness" (1QpHab 7:17—8:3).

The opposite of righteousness for the Essenes was "sin" (*ḥāṭā'*), which meant "missing the mark or goal" (of life), or "transgression" (*pešaʿ*), the violation of a commandment or a covenant, or "iniquity" (*ʿāwôn*), a guilty misdeed: "They will admit before God, 'Assuredly, we have sinned; we have done evil, we and our ancestors, walking contrary to the ordinances of the covenant'" (CD 20:28–29). "The Levites will recount all the iniquities of the Israelites, all of their guilty transgressions and their sins during the dominion of Belial" (1QS 1:22–24). Those who fail in this way were considered to be dominated by the Angel of Darkness, as was seen in the discussion of dualism. This opposition of righteousness and sin will be resolved only in the end-time, as various passages in the Thanksgiving Psalms make clear. For instance, "You protect those who serve You faithfully, so that their descendants are before You all the days. You have raised an everlasting name, forgiving offense, casting away all their iniquities, and giving them as an inheritance all the glory of Adam and an abundance of days" (1QH^a 4 [old 17]:14–15).

(d) *New Jerusalem.* Because the Essenes found fault with the priests who were serving in the Temple in Jerusalem, they refused to worship there with them. They considered not only the Temple but also the city itself to be contaminated. This is why most of them withdrew to the desert retreat at Qumran. Recalling the words of Isa 54:11–14, "O afflicted one, storm-tossed and uncomforted, lo, I shall set your stones in antimony and lay your foundations in sapphire. I shall make your pinnacles of agate, your gates of carbuncle, and all your walls of precious stones.…You will be far from oppression for you will not fear, and far from terror for it will not come near you," the Essenes understood these words as God's promise of a New Jerusalem. Imitating Ezekiel 40—48, the Essenes drew up elaborate sketches of the way the new city would be built. These sketches, too detailed to be quoted here, are found in 2QNJ (2Q24), 4QNJ^{a-b} (4Q554–555), 5QNJ (5Q15), and 11QNJ (11Q18). Related to these texts is 11QTemple^a 3–13, which gives the dimensions of the New Temple, as the Essenes wanted it to be constructed.

(e) *Astrology.* It is strange that the Essenes, who cherished many quite orthodox Jewish convictions and beliefs, would have also shown an interest in astrological aspects of human life. One document, at least, reveals such a conviction; it is called a "Brontologion," that is, a saying about thunder, 4QZodBront ar (4Q318). It is an Aramaic horoscopic text that has preserved the names of the twelve signs of the Zodiac and relates what will happen if it thunders on a given day: "…on the 29th and on the 30th, Libra. [Month of Tishri:] on the 1st and the 2d, Scorpio; on the 3d and 4th, Sagittarius; on the 5th, 6th, and 7th, Capricorn;…If it thunders in Taurus, here will revolutions against[   ]and affliction for the province, and a sword in the king's court.…If it thunders in Gemini, fear and distress from foreigners…" (1:8–9; 2 ii 69).[4]

This Brontologion, however, is not the only Qumran document that contains horoscopic details. There is also 4QHoroscope (4Q186), which interprets the meaning of an unnamed person's limbs: "His thighs are long and slender, and his toes are thin and long. So he is in the second column(?). His spirit has six parts in the house of light and three in the house of darkness. This is the sign in which he was born: the time of Taurus. He will be poor…" (1 ii 5–9).

There are also three fragmentary texts describing the newborn Noah, 4QBirthNoah^{a-c} (4Q534–536). Unfortunately, the description is broken and very fragmentary, but enough is found in one of them to show the meaning of marks on Noah's body: "...red is his hair, and he has moles on his [ ] , and tiny marks on his thighs [ ] different from each other. So he will know [ ]. In his youth he will be like one who knows nothing, until the time when he will read the three books" (4Q534 1:2–5).

The foregoing items reveal the main beliefs of the Essenes that are found in the Qumran scrolls. To them one has to add the practices of the sect, the main item of which is the celebration of their feast days according to the calendar used by it, reference to which is found in many writings. For instance, in 11QPs^a (11Q5) 27:4–8 a record of "David's Compositions" is given: "He wrote psalms: three thousand, six hundred; and songs to be sung at the altar over the continual offerings of each day, for all the days of the year: three hundred and sixty-four; and for the Sabbath offerings: fifty-two songs; and for the offerings of the first day of the months, for all the feast days, and for the Day of Atonement: thirty songs." Even though this is not a calendaric text, it reveals that the Essenes used a calendar that numbered only 364 days to the year.

This sort of year was not an Essene creation, because traces of the solar calendar have been found in writings that antedate the origin of their sect, for example, in the Book of the Luminaries in *1 Enoch* 74:12; and in the *Book of Jubilees* 6:30 ("Bid, then, the children of Israel to observe the years in accordance with this reckoning: three hundred and sixty-four days; for these will make a complete year"). *Jubilees* relates this solar calendar to the Jewish feast days, but *Enoch* does not; and the *Prologue of Jubilees* (1:29) even traces the origin of this calendar to an "angel of the Presence," who brought "tablets of the weeks of jubilees according to their years" to the Israelites.

There is a series of calendaric texts in QL that supply many details about this division of time and its relation to the Jewish feast days: 4QCalDocMA (4Q320), 4QCalDocMB (4Q321), 4QCalDocMC (4Q322), 4QCalDocE (4Q337); 6QCalDoc (6Q17). Still other texts relate this calendar to the Mishmarot, that is, "Watches," or the weekly rotation of priest groups who were to serve in the Temple (see 1 Chr 24:7–19): 4QMišmarotA (4Q322),

4QMišmarotB (4Q323), 4QMišmarotC (4Q324), 4QMišmarotD (4Q324a), 4QMišmarotE (4Q324c).

The solar calendar of 364 days divided the 12 months of the year into four groups of three months, each of which had 30, 30, and 31 days:

Days of the Week																
	I, IV, VII, X					II, V, VIII, XI					III, VI, IX, XII					
Wednesday	1	8	15	22	29		6	13	20	27		4	11	18	25	
Thursday	2	9	16	23	30		7	14	21	28		5	12	19	26	
Friday	3	10	17	24		1	8	15	22	29		6	13	20	27	
Saturday	4	11	18	25		2	9	16	23	30		7	14	21	28	
Sunday	5	12	19	26		3	10	17	24		1	8	15	22	29	
Monday	6	13	20	27		4	11	18	25		2	9	16	23	30	
Tuesday	7	14	21	28		5	12	19	26		3	10	17	24	31	
	(30)					(30)					(31)					

In following such a solar calendar, the Essenes set themselves apart from the rest of the Jews of their time, who were using a lunar calendar of 354 days to a year. The advantage of the 364-day calendar was that the feast days fell on the same day of the week every year, which would not have been true of the lunar calendar of 354 days. According to the latter, it would have been necessary to compute when the feast day would occur, and it was open to error in computation. The Manual of Discipline shows how important the calendar was to the Essene sect: "They shall not stray from any one of God's orders about their appointed times; they shall not advance their appointed times, and they shall not retard any of their feasts" (1QS 1:14–15); "To keep the Sabbath day in accordance with its exact interpretation, and feast days, and the day of fasting, in accordance with what was discovered by those who entered the new covenant in the land of Damascus" (CD 6:18–19). This calendaric issue was so important for the Essenes that they refused to worship in the Jerusalem Temple, where the priests serving there were following the lunar calendar. Given such an aversion to the Temple priests, it is surprising that the Essenes still had regulations governing the Mishmarot, for the rotation of priestly service in the Temple. Undoubtedly, they had such regulations in the hope that the Temple service might one day be conducted according to the solar calendar that they preferred.

There are many other aspects of this calendar that affected the lives of the Essenes and their leaders, such as the Teacher of Righteousness, who was persecuted by the Wicked Priest on the Day of Atonement, as we have already learned (see pp. 34–35 above).

IX

THE SCROLLS AND CHRISTIANITY:
John the Baptist, Jesus of Nazareth, New Testament

Having discussed the impact that the discovery of the Qumran Scrolls has had on the history of ancient Palestinian Judaism and on the study of the OT, I turn now to another area where the scrolls have had great influence, viz., on early Christianity. It is not surprising that the scrolls have had such influence, because Christianity was born in ancient Judea during the time that the Essene Jews lived at Qumran and in towns and villages throughout Judea.

In approaching this topic, I must issue a warning at the outset. This topic is not being discussed in any apologetic sense, as if it were more or less important than it really is. There is, first of all, a need to be aware of a Christian tendency, often subconscious, to color details in these thoroughly Jewish scrolls or magnify them unduly in a Christian sense. Second, some years ago, shortly after the publication of the first scrolls from Cave 1, the Jewish scholar Samuel Sandmel warned those who were studying them about "Parallelomania."[1] Parallels there are indeed; but perhaps the comment should be, "So what?" The parallels may be sheer coincidence. Third, one often sees quoted the dictum of E. R. Goodenough about parallels: A parallel by definition consists of straight lines in the same plane that never meet, however far they are extended in any direction. That definition, however, is derived from mathematics and is being applied to literature. To repeat the dictum as if it closes all discussion or absolves one from investigating the literary relationship of authors to some sources is only a form of obscurantism—

something little better than parallelomania or pan-Qumranism. It also enables one to avoid asking the question, when a *literary* parallel might cease to be such and prove actually to be a *contact*.

There is, though, an a priori likelihood of contacts of the Essenes with the early Christian movement, even if it has to face the mysterious silence of the NT about such Jews. In the NT, we read about the Pharisees and the Sadducees, two of the *haireseis*, "sects," that Josephus mentions (*Life* 1 §10), but never about Essenes, the Jewish sect that he describes in greatest detail. What parallels or contacts do emerge between QL and NT are found mostly in the writings of Christians of the second or third generation, and they touch on secondary elements in the NT, scarcely on its main Christian message, the good news of what Jesus of Nazareth has done for humanity.

Before looking at such parallels or contacts, I have to take up the question of John the Baptist and Jesus of Nazareth and their possible relations to the Essenes of Qumran.

1. John the Baptist

John, the son of the priest Zechariah and Elizabeth (Luke 1:5), is mentioned nowhere in any of Qumran Scrolls or in any of the Dead Sea Scrolls (in the broad sense), even though he is known to have been a contemporary of the Qumran Essenes. The Jewish historian Josephus knew of John and reported that some Jews claimed that God had destroyed the army of Herod Antipas, the tetrarch of Galilee, "because of the execution of John, called the Baptist" (*Ant.* 18.5.2 §§116–19; see Mark 6:16–29, the Gospel account of John's death).

According to the Lucan account of the Baptist, he never served in the Temple, as did his father, Zechariah, but "lived rather out in the desert until the day he was manifested to Israel" (1:80). Moreover, "in the fifteenth year of the reign of Tiberius, when Pontius Pilate was prefect of Judea,…a message came from God to John, the son of Zechariah, in the desert; and he moved into the region all around the Jordan to preach a baptism of repentance for the forgiveness of sins" (3:1–3); then Luke quotes Isa 40:3 and applies it to the beginning of John's mission, "A voice of someone crying out in the desert, 'Make ready the way of the Lord, make straight the paths for Him.'" This account raises the question, What was John doing in the desert before God's message came to him? Could he have been associated with the Essenes of Qumran until that message came that called him to break off from them?

A number of reasons make it plausible that John was, indeed, among the Essenes at Qumran until called by God for a new career.

(a) A long-standing tradition has identified the spot of John's baptizing along the Jordan River (Luke 3:3) as the site of a later Greek Orthodox monastic settlement, "Deir Mar Yuḥannan," which preserves John's name. It is within walking distance of the Essene community center at Khirbet Qumran (about four miles away).

(b) All four Gospels quote Isa 40:3 ("the voice of someone crying out in the desert...") to explain John's presence there. The Manual of Discipline quotes the same passage of Isaiah to explain why the Essenes are in the desert (1QS 8:12–18). There the reason for their desert retreat is explained as "the study of the Law" (8:15), whereas John awaited God's call in the desert.

(c) John was called by God "to preach a baptism of repentance for the forgiveness of sins" (Luke 3:3). Josephus has recorded the same: "...to join in baptism...this washing would not be acceptable as pardon for sins..., unless the soul had been cleansed previously through upright conduct" (*Ant.* 18.5.2 §116). John continued, "I am baptizing you with water, but someone more powerful than I is coming....He will baptize you with a holy Spirit and with fire" (Luke 3:16).

A similar washing for a spiritual purpose is found in the Manual of Discipline, where it is said that one entering the covenant was entering "into water": "Let him not enter the water, to use the purification of holy men, for he will not be purified, unless he turns from his wickedness" (1QS 5:13–14). In this way, the Essenes thought of their ritual washings in relation to sin. It is not identical with John's baptism or preaching; but his conception of baptism could well have developed from theirs. Again, John's baptism was explained as related to water, Spirit, and fire (Luke 3:16); this is similar to a different passage in the Manual of Discipline, which reads:

> Then [at the season of visitation, when the truth of the world will appear] God will purge by His truth all the deeds of human beings, refining [by fire] for Himself some of mankind to remove every evil spirit from the midst of their flesh, to cleanse them with a holy Spirit from all wicked practices, and to sprinkle them with a spirit of truth like purifying water. (1QS 4:20–21)

(d) Josephus records that the Essenes adopted the sons of other people, "while yet pliable and docile" and molded them according to their own principles (*J.W.* 2.8.2 §120). Such an adoption could explain why John, after the death of his elderly parents, would have spent some time in the desert at Qumran. Josephus also mentions how he himself had lived for a while among the Essenes, before he left them to spend three years in the desert with Bannus, a hermit (*Life* 2 §§10–11). A similar short sojourn with the Essenes of Qumran could also have been John's.

Such reasons as these make it a plausible hypothesis—nothing more—that John the Baptist lived with the Essenes at Qumran for a short time, until God called him to a different career. One factor, however, may militate against its plausibility: John was the son of a priest who served in the Jerusalem Temple, and given the Essene disapproval of that priesthood (see 1QpHab 9:4–7; 4QpNah [4Q169] 3–4 i 11), one wonders whether they would have adopted such a son.

2. Jesus of Nazareth

There is no mention of Jesus of Nazareth anywhere in the QL. Since most of the scrolls date from the first century B.C., it is not surprising that he is not named in any of them. Those that are dated palaeographically to the first century A.D. come usually from such an early time in that century that there is little likelihood that they would say anything about him.

That Jesus knew of the Essenes of Qumran is not unlikely. That he taught some of the same things that they espoused is not impossible, but there is no way of being certain about either question, mainly because the Essenes are not mentioned in the NT.

It has been suggested at times that one or other of Jesus' sayings recorded in the Gospels implies his awareness of the Qumran community. For example, Jesus speaks of the coming of false Messiahs, saying, "If they say to you, 'Look, he is in the desert,' do not go out. If they say, 'He is in the inner rooms,' do not believe it" (Matt 24:24). Could the Matthean Jesus be referring to the Qumran community and its messianic beliefs? It is possible, but how can anyone be sure that he is referring to a Messiah awaited by the Essenes? Similarly, in Matt 19:12 Jesus mentions those who "have made themselves eunuchs for the sake of the kingdom of heaven." Is he alluding to the celibate Essenes of Qumran? Possibly, but not certainly; and that would have to be said about any saying that might be similar to an Essene tenet.

There are some students of the scrolls who have identified individuals mentioned in them as John the Baptist or Jesus of Nazareth. For instance, an Australian, Barbara E. Thiering, claimed that she had found evidence in the scrolls that John the Baptist was the Teacher of Righteousness and that Jesus was the "rival leader" (does she mean the "Wicked Priest"?) of the group of Jews that broke off from John and his followers and went into schism.[2]

3. Early Christian Community

One of the names found in the NT for the primitive Christian community is "the Way" (*hē hodos*), in Acts 9:2; 19:9, 23; 22:4; 24:14, 23. Commentators on Acts have said either that they could not find out where this name came from or that it was a shortening of "the way of the Lord/God," as in Acts 18:25–26. *Hadderek*, "the Way," however, occurs a number of times at the designation of the Essene community at Qumran: *tikkûnê hadderek*, "the regulations of the Way" (1QS 9:21); *lĕbôḥôrê derek*, "those who choose the Way" (1QS 9:17–18); *sôrĕrê derek*, "those who turn aside from the Way" (CD 2:6). This evidence might suggest that early Christians, in using "the Way" as a name for their members, were imitating the Essene designation of their community.

The "overseer" or "bishop" (*episkopos*) in the Christian community is a title usually explained as borrowed from contemporary Hellenism, where it designates a market overseer (e.g., Plato, *Leges* VIII, §849a). *Episkopos* occurs a number of times in the LXX, mostly in a secular sense, but occasionally as the designation of the "overseer" of priests and levites (Neh 11:9, 14, 22) or of the Temple (2 Kgs 11:18). Such usage could easily explain the Christian adoption of the title. However, in QL one finds *mĕbaqqēr* with the same meaning and as a superior or official in the Essene community: "the overseer will record it personally" (CD 9:19); "the overseer will instruct him in the exact meaning of the Law" (CD 13:6); similarly 4Q265 4 ii 6, 8; 4Q266 5 i 4; 5Q13 4:1. Unfortunately, no one can say to what extent this Essene usage might have influenced the Christian understanding of *episkopos* as "bishop."

In the Acts of the Apostles, Luke recounts the story of Ananias and Sapphira (Acts 5:1–11), the early Christians in Jerusalem, who deceived the rest of the Christians there. Luke has described the Jewish Christians themselves as "a company" of one heart and one soul, who never possessed anything as their own, but shared "everything in common" (Acts 4:32). But Ananias sold a piece of his property with his wife's knowledge, put part of the profit from it at the apostles' feet, and kept the rest. This deceit became known to Peter, who realized that Satan had filled the hearts of Ananias and Sapphira. When they realized that their deed was known, they dropped dead.

The common life that these Jewish Christians were living was like that of the Qumran Essenes, who held their possessions in common and cared for each other from their common profits:

> This is the rule of the Many, to provide for all their needs: the salary of two days each month at least, which they will place in the hand of the Overseer and the Judges. From it they will give to the injured, and with it they will support the needy and the poor, the elder who is bent over, the afflicted, the prisoner of a foreign people. (CD 14:12–17)

But the Essenes also had a regulation that said, "If anyone is found among them who has lied knowingly concerning possessions, he shall be excluded from the pure food of the Many for a year, and they shall withhold a quarter of his food" (1QS 6:24–25). This regulation is similar to the account about Ananias and Sapphira in Acts, even if it is not so rigorous in its penalty.

4. New Testament

In Qumran Cave 7, nineteen fragments were found, all written in Greek; two were biblical texts (7Q1: Exod 28:4–7; 7Q2: Epistle of Jeremy [Baruch 6]:43–44) and the rest (7Q3–19) remained unidentified. In 1972, José O'Callaghan published an article in which he claimed to identify eight of the fragments (7Q4–l0, 15) as quotations of NT verses. He considered 7Q4 to be part of 1 Tim 3:16; 4:1, 3; 7Q5 as Mark 6:52–53; 7Q6/l as Mark 4:28; 7Q6/2 as Acts 27:38; 7Q7 as Mark 12:17; 7Q8 as Jas 1:23–24; 7Q9 as Rom 5:11–12; 7Q10 as 2 Pet 1:15; and 7Q15 as Mark 6:48.[3]

If O'Callaghan had been right, one would have had to change the interpretation of many of the finds at Qumran and revise the dating of many NT writings: for example, Christians would have been among the people resident at Qumran; 2 Peter would have been written before the fall of Jerusalem.

Many scholars and students of the Qumran scrolls, however, remained quite skeptical about his identification, because most of the 7Q fragments are so small and contain so few letters that they almost defy identification. O'Callaghan continued to insist on the NT identification until his death.[4] He found, nevertheless, a few people to support his identification, chief among whom was a German scholar, Carsten P. Thiede.[5] More recently it has been discovered that some of these fragments are a Greek translation of *1 Enoch*.

X

THE SCROLLS AND THE WRITINGS OF PAUL OF TARSUS

The evidence about the contact of Jesus of Nazareth or of his followers with the Qumran Essenes is minimal, but the evidence about the contact with the Essenes of those Christians who wrote about him and the movement he started is quite different. The literary parallels or contacts increase with the later writers of the NT books, which is part of the otherwise strange silence in the NT about the Essenes.

The chief difference between the QL and the NT lies in the Christian gospel, the good news of what Jesus of Nazareth achieved for humanity in his life, passion, death, and resurrection. There is nothing like that news in the QL. An important secondary difference, however, is the eschatology of the two groups. The Essenes, who seem to have been convinced that they were living already in the end-time, were looking forward predominantly to the end of that period, to the coming of a Prophet and the Messiahs of Aaron and Israel and to the final battle of the sons of light against the sons of darkness. The early Christians, however, who also may be thought of as already living in the end-time, predominantly looked backward to Jesus of Nazareth as the Messiah who has already come.

The earliest NT writer who wrote about Jesus was not one of the evangelists, but Paul of Tarsus. Even before any of the Gospels, the narratives of what Jesus did and said, were composed, Paul was interpreting the meaning of what Jesus did and said. So the interpretation preceded the narrative. Paul is known to Christians of a later date from his letters and the account of his ministry that Luke later composed in the Acts of the Apostles. The seven uncontested letters of Paul (1 Thessalonians, Galatians, Philippians, 1–2 Corin-

97

thians, Romans, and Philemon) date from A.D. 51 to 57/58 and are therefore earlier than the Gospel accounts, which date from A.D. 65 to 95. Some of the sayings of Jesus are preserved in Paul's writings (1 Cor 7:10 [prohibition of divorce]; 1 Cor 11:23–25 [institution of the Eucharist]), and many traces of what Paul called "the story of the cross" (1 Cor 1:18).

Among Paul's writings, one finds a good number of passages that contain parallels or literary contacts with the writings of the Essenes, but it remains a mystery how one should account for them. All the Pauline letters that have been preserved are written in Greek, and yet the echoes of Hebrew and Aramaic formulations are part of that mystery.[1]

Essene Echoes in Pauline Writings

1. Generic Theological Teaching

Various features of Pauline theology have been detected as similar to that of the Essenes: justification by grace, interpretation of Hab 2:4, curse of the law, lists of vices and virtues, and dualism.

(a) Justification by Grace. Paul derived this important teaching partly from the OT and its notion of the righteousness of God and the corresponding righteousness of human beings (as in Ps 35:24; 1 Kgs 8:32). To this basic OT notion Paul added "by grace through faith." This development echoes in part the teaching of justification by the Essenes. A succinct summation of this teaching is found in the Manual of Discipline and in the Thanksgiving Psalms:

> As for me, I belong to wicked humanity, to the assembly of perverse flesh; my iniquities, my transgressions, my sins together with the wickedness of my heart belong to the assembly doomed to worms and walking in darkness. No human being sets his own path or directs his own steps, for to God alone belongs the judgment of him, and from His hand comes perfection of way....And I, if I stagger, God's grace is my salvation forever. If I stumble

because of a sin of the flesh, my judgment is according to the righteousness of God, which stands forever....In His mercy He has drawn me close (to Him), and with His favors will He render judgment of me. In His righteous fidelity He has judged me; in His bounteous goodness He expiates all my iniquities, and in His righteousness He cleanses me of human defilement and of human sinfulness, that I may praise God for His righteousness and the Most High for His majesty. (1QS 11:9–15)

Who is righteous before You, when he is judged? No answer can be made to Your rebuke! All human glory is like the wind, and no one is able to stand before Your wrath. Yet You bring all Your faithful children to pardon before You, to cleanse them of their transgressions with much goodness and in the abundance of Your mercy. (1QH^{a}15 [old 7]:28–30)

As for me, I know that righteousness does not belong to a human being, nor perfection of way to a son of man. To God Most High belong all the deeds of righteousness, whereas the path of a human being is not set firm....And I said, "It is because of my transgressions that I have been abandoned far from Your covenant. But when I recalled Your mighty hand along with the abundance of Your mercy, then I was restored, and I stood up; my spirit strengthened my stance against blows, because I have based myself on Your graces and on the abundance of Your mercy. For You expiate iniquity to cleanse a human being from guilt by Your righteousness." (1QH^a 12 [old 4]:30–31, 35–38)

Here one sees how the Essenes developed their understanding of God's righteousness and His activity in acquitting or justifying human beings. The Essenes have added to the OT teaching an emphasis on God's grace and mercy. This is part of the Pauline addition, but not the whole, because there is no mention of "faith" (*'ĕmûnāh*) in any of the passages just cited that summarize the

Essene teaching on justification. For Paul, that status of a human being standing before the tribunal of God the Judge and hearing the verdict, "Innocent, not guilty!" comes about only as a result of what Christ Jesus did for humanity in his life, death, resurrection, and exaltation: "For all alike have sinned and fall short of the glory of God; yet all are justified freely by His grace through the redemption that comes in Christ Jesus. Through his blood God has presented him as a means of expiating sin for all who have faith" (Rom 3:23–25). And again, "It is also going to be credited to us who believe in Him who raised from the dead Jesus our Lord, who was handed over (to death) for our trespasses and raised for our justification" (Rom 4:24–25). Hence, "now…God's righteousness has been disclosed" (Rom 3:21).

Apart from the references to faith and the Christ-event, the Pauline formulation sounds remarkably like the Essene teaching. When both the Essenes and Paul use the phrase "the righteousness of God," they are expressing succinctly a good OT teaching, even though the exact phrase is not found in the Hebrew OT. The closest formula is found in Ps 98:2, which speaks of "His righteousness" (*ṣidqātô*), but it is not the same two words. Compare the Essene formulas, *ṣidqāt ʾĒl* (1QS 11:12), or *ṣedeq ʾĒl* (1QM 4:6); and the Pauline formula, *dikaiosynē theou* (Rom 1:17; 3:21).

(b) Interpretation of Hab 2:4. Both the Essenes and Paul interpreted this text in related ways. The OT text itself reads, "The one who is righteous shall find life through his fidelity." In the original context, these words are part of God's reply to the prophet's complaint about the oppression of Judah coming from awaited Chaldean invaders: the righteous Judahite will preserve his life by fidelity to God.

The Essene commentary on this verse interprets the saying: "The meaning of it concerns all those observing the Law in the house of Judah, whom God will free from the house of judgment because of their effort and their loyalty to the Teacher of Righteousness" (1QpHab 8:1–3). In this interpretation, one finds an important development beyond the OT meaning, because these pre-Christian Palestinian Jews have understood Habakkuk's words to refer to a person: the prophet's words are addressed to "observers of the Law" and relate their "effort" and "loyalty" to the Teacher of

Righteousness. So this Essene interpretation proves to be transitional between what Habakkuk meant and what Paul will make of it.

In Rom 1:17, Paul quotes Hab 2:4, "In it [the gospel] is revealed the righteousness of God, through faith and for faith, as it stands written, 'The one who is righteous shall find life through faith'" (see also Gal 3:11). For all its similarity to the Essene understanding of Hab 2:4, this Pauline use of it goes beyond their use of it. First, because Paul understands 'ĕmûnāh not merely as "loyalty," but as "faith" in the Christian sense, that is, faith in the risen Christ. Second, because Paul takes "life" not merely as deliverance from the coming oppression of Chaldean invaders (as in Habakkuk) or rescue from the house of judgment (as in the Essene commentary), but as "life in Christ Jesus," that is, a share in the risen life of Christ (as in Rom 6:4b). Third, because Paul has omitted the possessive pronoun, "*his* fidelity," he enables *pistis* to take on the new Christian connotation of "faith" (in the risen Christ).

(c) The Curse of the Law. Still another echo of an Essene interpretation of an OT passage is heard in Paul's letter to the Galatians, where he cites an OT text to show how Christ has redeemed humanity from the curse of the Law, "having become a curse for us, for it stands written, 'Cursed be everyone who is hanged on a tree'" (Gal 3:13, quoting Deut 21:23). Commentators on Galatians have tried often to explain how that verse of Deuteronomy would be applicable to Christ *crucified* because, in its original context, it refers to the hanging or impaling of the dead body of an executed criminal as a consummate disgrace and a deterrent to further crime. *Per se*, it has nothing to do with crucifixion.

Now, however, it is known that Paul was quoting that verse of Deuteronomy, as it came to be understood by Palestinian Jews in the Roman period, when crucifixion was a common punishment for crimes. One finds such an understanding of Deut 21:22–23 in the Qumran Pesher on Nahum and in the Temple Scroll from Qumran Cave 11.

The first passage contains a commentary on Nah 2:12–14, where the prophet was describing the plundering of Nineveh and the terror caused thereby for its Assyrian inhabitants, as the Lord of Hosts saw to its destruction in 612 B.C. The Essenes applied the prophet's words of vv. 12–13 rather to Judea:

The lion tears enough for its cubs (and) strangles prey for its lionesses. The meaning of it concerns the Lion of Wrath, who struck by means of his nobles and his counsellors....*He fills with prey his cave and his den with torn flesh.* The meaning of it concerns the Lion of Wrath, who has found a crime punishable by death in the Seekers-after-Smooth-Things, whom he hangs alive on a tree, as it was thus done in Israel from of old, for of one hanged alive on the tree, it [Scripture] reads: *"Behold I am against you says the Lord of Hosts and I will burn in smoke your abundance and the sword shall devour your young lions and I will cut off from the land its prey...."* (4QpNah [4Q169] 3–4 i 4–9)

Line 2 of the same passage mentions "Demetrius, the king of Greece, who sought to enter Jerusalem on the advice of the Seekers-after-Smooth-Things." These words refer to the Seleucid ruler, Demetrios III Eukairos (95–78 B.C.). Adversaries of the bellicose Sadducee high priest Alexander Jannaeus (in office 103–76 B.C.), who in this text is called "the Lion of Wrath," had begged Demetrius to come to their assistance. They are the ones called "the Seekers-after-Smooth-Things" and are identified usually as Pharisees. Demetrius marched against Jerusalem, but he did not take the city. Eventually, Alexander Jannaeus, "the Lion of Wrath," regained control. Josephus recounts how he then "did a thing that was as cruel as could be:...he ordered some 800 of the Jews to be crucified and slaughtered their children and wives before the eyes of the still living wretches" (*Ant.* 13.14.2 §380; *J.W.* 1.4.5 §§93–98). This is the incident to which 4QpNah 3–4 i 4–9 refers.

The editor of the Temple Scroll, Y. Yadin, has related a passage of that scroll to the text of the Pesher of Nahum just quoted. It reads:

If a man has informed against his people and betrays his people to a foreign nation, and has done such evil to his people, you will hang him on a tree, and he will die. On the evidence of two witnesses and on the evidence of three witnesses, he will be put to death, and they will hang him on a tree. If a man has committed a crime punishable by death and has fled to the midst of Gentiles and has cursed his people and the children of Israel, *you will hang him too on a tree* and he will die. *Their bodies will not spend the night on the tree but you will bury them that very day, for what is hanged on a tree is accursed by God* and human beings; *and you will not defile the land that I am giving to you for an inheritance.* (11QTemple[a] [11Q19] 64:6–13)

This passage of 11Q19 interprets Deut 21:22–23, which is quoted (in the italicized words) and applied to two capital crimes: treason (of different forms) and evasion of due process of law. The first of these crimes is exemplified by the actions of the Seekers-after-Smooth-Things, who invited Demetrius to come to take Jerusalem. The interpretation of "hanging on a tree" as crucifixion has been contested at times, but the combination of the wording of these two Qumran texts, especially "hanging alive on a tree," together with the testimony of Josephus (quoted above), makes it practically certain that the punishment is crucifixion.[2] Such an interpretation of these Qumran passages confirms Paul's application of the curse of the Law in Gal 3:13 to Christ crucified.

2. Specific Literary Themes

Among the literary themes that the Essenes and Paul use in common or in parallel, one has to consider the lists of vices and virtues, dualism, and testimonia.

(a) Lists of Vices and Virtues. When Paul describes the plight of pagans who live without the Christian gospel, he lists in Rom 1:29–31 the vices to which they have been degraded: "They became filled with every sort of wickedness: evil, greed, and malice; they were full of envy, murder, strife, craftiness, and spite." In Rom 13:13 and Gal 5:19–21, one finds other lists of the "deeds of darkness" and "of the flesh," which stand in contrast to "the fruit of the Spirit": "love, joy, peace, patience, goodness, fidelity, gentleness, self-control" (Gal 5:22–23). Paul seems to have adopted lists that were already composed. If that impression is not correct, there is at

least a similarity of genre in his lists to what one reads in 1QS
4:9–11:

> To the spirit of iniquity belong greed, sloth in the service
> of justice, wickedness, deceit, pride, haughtiness of heart,
> dishonesty, trickery, cruelty, impudence, hypocrisy, impa-
> tience, much folly, zealous arrogance, abominable deeds
> of lust, and lewd ways in the service of indecency, a blas-
> phemous tongue, blindness of eyes, dullness of ears, stiff-
> ness of neck, hardness of heart, so that man walks on all
> the paths of darkness and guile.

Such vices are not the same as those in the Pauline lists, but
they at least manifest the same literary genre as his. To the list of
vices corresponds a list of virtues, which belong to "the spirit of
fidelity":

> a spirit-of meekness, patience, generous compassion,
> everlasting goodness; intelligence, mighty wisdom that
> trusts in all the deeds of God and depends on His abun-
> dant mercy; a spirit of knowledge about every design of
> action, zeal for righteous regulations, a holy intention
> with a firm purpose, abundant kindness toward all the
> children of truth; admirable purity that abominates all
> unclean idols, unpretentious conduct with prudence in
> everything; and concealment of the truth of the myster-
> ies of knowledge. (1QS 4:3–6)

(b) Dualism. This characteristic of Essene life has been discussed already, but now there is the comparison of it with the few
places where it occurs in Pauline writings. In his earliest letter, Paul
tells the Thessalonians, "You are all sons of light and sons of the
day; we are not of the night or of darkness. Therefore, let us not
sleep, as others do, but let us keep awake and be sober" (1 Thess
5:5–6). Similarly Paul exhorts the Roman Christians, "Let us cast
off the deeds of darkness and don the armor of light, that we may
conduct ourselves with decency as befits the daylight" (Rom
13:12–13). In the letter to the Ephesians, the author writes simi-

larly, "For you were once darkness, but now you are light in the Lord; walk, then, as children of light" (5:8). Likewise, "Satan disguises himself as an angel of light" (2 Cor 11:14).

Compare the Essene instruction: "to love all the sons of light, each one according to his lot in God's design, and to hate all the sons of darkness, each one according to his guilt" (1QS 1:9–10). "The sons of light and the lot of darkness shall battle together with God's might" (1QM 1:11). "In the hand of the Angel of Darkness is complete domination of the sons of deceit; they walk on paths of darkness" (1QS 3:20–21).

(c) Testimonia. By "testimonia" is meant a collection of OT citations that supports a theme that needs to be emphasized. Paul provides a good example of such a collection in Rom 3:10–18, where he shows that all human beings, Jews and Greeks alike, are sinners:

> As it stands written, "No one is upright, no, not one"; "no one has understanding; no one searches for God. All have turned away, all have become depraved. No one does good, not even one." "Their throats are open graves; with their tongues they have practiced deceit"; "the poison of asps lies behind their lips." "Their mouths are full of cursing and bitterness." "Swift are their feet to shed blood. Ruin and wretchedness strew their paths. The path of peace they have not known." "Fear of God is not before their eyes."

Seven OT verses are strung together from Qoh 7:20; Pss 14:1–3; 5:10; 140:4; 10:7; Isa 59:7–8 (or Prov 1:16), and Ps 36:2. They have a catchword bonding, which mentions parts of the body: throat, tongue, lips, mouth, feet, and eyes—the parts of the body that are involved in committing sin.

This literary form has a counterpart in the Essene text called 4QTestim (4Q175), where Deut 5:28–29; 18:18–19 (= Samaritan Pentateuch Exod 20:21); Num 24:15–17; Deut 33:8–11; Josh 6:26; and 4QpsJosh are strung together in a similar way.

(d) Angels. Earlier in this survey of Essene beliefs, it was seen how the sectarians were convinced that they were living in the sight of God's angels, who were not to be exposed to human defects or deformities, as in 1QSa (1Q28a) 2:3–9 ("for the angels of holiness are in their congregation"); similarly in 1QM 7:4–6. The same notion is found in 1 Cor 11:10, where Paul insists that a woman praying publicly in a sacred assembly should cover her head "because of the angels." Earlier in the same passage Paul argued that the uncovered head of a woman in such a situation was like a shorn or shaved head, a disgraceful sight (11:6). The angels were not to be exposed to such a human sight; in this view Paul seems to have agreed with the Essenes of Qumran.

3. Specific Words

There are a number of significant Greek words and titles that Paul uses, which now find their counterparts in the Hebrew or Aramaic texts of Qumran.

(a) "The Lord." Rudolf Bultmann once wrote that "the Kyrios-cult originated on Hellenistic soil. Judaism, at any rate, never entitled the Messiah 'Lord.' At the very outset the un-modified expression 'the Lord' is unthinkable in Jewish usage. 'Lord' used of God is always given some modifier; we read: 'the Lord of heaven and earth,' 'our Lord' and similar expressions."[3]

Now, however, it is clear that Essene Jewish usage did use the absolute form of the title for God. In 4QEn^b (4Q202) 1 iv 5 (= *1 Enoch* 10:8) we read, "To Gabriel the Lord (*Māryā'*) said, 'Go to....'" Again, in 11QtgJob (11Q10) 24:6–7 (= Job 34:12), Elihu asks, "Now then, will God really do evil, and will the Lord (*Mārē'*) pervert justice?" Note the parallelism of "God" and "the Lord," which makes the usage unmistakable. So it was hardly "unthinkable in Jewish usage."

(b) "Works of the Law." The Greek phrase *erga nomou* as Paul uses it sounds like a Jewish slogan. Certainly, it was not a Pauline creation, but was part of the Palestinian Jewish teaching on the pursuit of a righteous status in God's sight. Yet it is never found in the OT (not even in 2 Chr 17:4; Isa 66:18; Sir 16:12, which have similar-sounding expressions), nor in later rabbinic literature. Now, however, it has turned up in QL. In 4QFlor (4Q174) 1–2 i 6–7, we read, "He proposed to build for Him a man-made sanctuary in which sacrifices would be made to Him, and that there would be before Him works of the Law (*ma'ăśê tôrāh*)." Similarly in the Halakhic Letter, 4QMMT C 27 (4Q398 2 ii 3), "We have also written to you some of the works of the Law (*miqṣat ma'ăśê hattôrāh*) which we believe are good for you and for your people." Related to this slogan are the words "his deeds in relation to the Law" (*ma'ăśāyw battôrāh*, 1QS 6:18). So when Paul singled out this phrase and criticized the use made of it by his former coreligionists, he knew whereof he was speaking.

4. 2 Cor 6:14—7:1

This Pauline paragraph is remarkable for the role that it plays in 2 Corinthians. It reads:

> Do not be misyoked with unbelievers. What partnership can uprightness have with iniquity? Or what fellowship can light have with darkness? What harmony can there be between Christ and Beliar? Or what part can a believer have with an unbeliever? What agreement has the temple of God with idols? For we are the temple of the living God; as God has said, "I shall dwell among them and move about among them, and I shall be their God and they will be my people. Therefore, come forth from them, and separate from them, says the Lord; touch nothing that is unclean"; then "I shall welcome you." And "I shall become a father to you; and you will be my sons and daughters, says the Lord Almighty." Since we have such promises, dear friends, let us purify ourselves from all that can taint body and spirit, and let us perfect our holiness in the fear of God.

This admonition to make no compromise with iniquity appears so abruptly that it breaks the sequence of thought between 6:13 and 7:2, between Paul's plea that the Corinthians "widen their hearts" (6:13) and "Open your hearts to us" (7:2). Because of this break, commentators have queried at times whether the paragraph might be an interpolation. Now that many of the phrases and ideas have turned up in QL, one wonders whether it is really a Pauline composition or a reworking of a Qumran paragraph.

The features in the Pauline paragraph that sound like echoes of Qumran phrases or ideas are the following: (a) the triple dualistic pairs: uprightness and iniquity, light and darkness, Christ and Beliar; (b) opposition to idols; (c) concept of the temple of God; (d) separation from impurity; and (e) the concatenation of OT texts.

Yet each of these features has counterparts in QL, and some of them have been discussed already in earlier parts of this book (e.g., dualism, temple of God, testimonia [= concatenation of OT texts]). Such similarities suggest that the paragraph in 6:14—7:1 is a reworked Essene composition that has been interpolated into 2 Corinthians.[4]

XI

THE SCROLLS AND
JOHANNINE WRITINGS

By "Johannine Writings" I mean the Gospel according to John and the three Johannine Epistles. Even though the Apocalypse (or Book of Revelation) is attributed to John, I shall treat that writing in the next chapter, along with other Christian writings of the NT.

The Gospel according to John, the fourth of the canonical Gospels, was hardly a second-century composition, as has been maintained at times. The Rylands Papyrus (P^{52}), containing parts of John 18:31–33, 37–38, is dated palaeographically to A.D. 100–125, which shows that the Gospel was already in existence at the end of the first Christian century. It is dated commonly to the last decade, A.D. 90–95, and not earlier. The Fourth Gospel is not a reformulation of the Christian good news in philosophical terms, despite its emphasis in the prologue on the *Logos* and its allegedly Platonic view of the world ("above...below," ideal vs. real). It contains rather a heavily Jewish Christian formulation that has embedded a primitive tradition about Jesus of Nazareth, along with a clear dependence on OT ideas, customs, and feasts. Hence, it is a late first-century *meditative reminiscence* of what Jesus once did and said.

The Johannine Epistles are a different sort of writing, but they contain many of the same ideas and formulations as the Johannine Gospel, especially the First Epistle. It is a matter of debate among Johannine interpreters whether all three epistles were written by the same author, but that does not concern us now.

As will be seen below, the Johannine Gospel and Epistles manifest contacts with Essene writings that are not just random parallels. It is not known, however, where or how such a contact took place. Ephesus has been regarded traditionally as the place of

composition of the Fourth Gospel, and because the Acts of the
Apostles speaks of disciples of John the Baptist in Ephesus (Acts
18:25—19:5), it has been suggested that the contact was made
through such disciples in Ephesus. A recent commentator on the
Gospel, however, has proposed rather that its author "was more
likely to have been an Essene," who was converted.[1]

A positive supporter of the contacts has been R. E. Brown, who
wrote extended commentaries on the Fourth Gospel and Johannine
Epistles.[2] He was a pioneer in the study of such contacts.[3]

Not every student of the Fourth Gospel admits that there are
contacts between it and Essene literature. Some would admit only
an extremely meager relationship; others insist that it is a mistaken
hypothesis. Most outspoken among the latter has been R. J.
Bauckham of the University of St Andrews in Scotland.[4] He has
maintained that the use of light/darkness imagery in the Johannine
writings and QL "exhibits far more impressive dissimilarities than
has been noticed in the scholarly enthusiasm for drawing conclu-
sions from the comparatively unimpressive similarities." For this
reason, it is necessary to study once again the evidence of the contacts or parallels and not limit them to the "light/darkness imagery,"
as Bauckham does.

The evidence can be discussed under five headings: Creation,
Dualism, Spirit of Truth, Love of Community Members, and Other
Miscellaneous Parallels.[5]

1. Creation

The OT teaching about God as creator of "the heavens and
the earth" is not only repeated in QL and the Fourth Gospel, but
it is developed in a strikingly similar formulation: "From the God
of knowledge exists everything that is and will come to be" (1QS
3:15); "through His knowledge, everything will come to be, and
everything that exists He establishes in His design, and nothing is
made apart from Him" (1QS 11:11); "and apart from Your will,
nothing is made" (1QS 11:17). See also 1QHª 9 [old 1]:7–8; 18 [old
10]:2, 9. This formulation is comparable to that of the prologue of
John's Gospel, where it is said of the *Logos*, "Word": "All things

came to be through Him, and apart from Him not a thing came into being" (1:3). What is important here is not only the reaffirmation of the OT teaching but the double formulation of it, in a positive and negative mode, as in the Qumran texts quoted. One does not expect to find in QL a mention of the *Logos* in the Christian meaning, but the activity ascribed there to God's knowledge or will, both positively and negatively, is attributed by the Christian evangelist to the Word.

2. Dualism

Even before the discovery of the Qumran Scrolls, commentators on John's Gospel had studied the elaborate dualism that one encounters in it and in the Johannine Epistles. There are seven pairs of opposites: death and life, flesh and spirit, light and darkness, truth and lies/error, above and below, earthly and heavenly, Jesus/God/Father and the world. Hence the dualism is not limited to the opposition of light and darkness, as Bauckham would have the reader believe.

The sevenfold dualism of the Johannine writings has no parallel in QL, where one finds rather a dualism that views human beings and their role in the universe as subject to opposing principles of good and evil, which have been adjusted to Judeo-Christian monotheism. They are controlled by God. Moreover, this dualism is a development beyond OT teaching, in which agents of evil seduce or try to seduce human beings (the serpent of Genesis 3, or Satan in Job 1, or wicked people), but that OT opposition is not always presented in dualistic fashion.

The Essenes extended the OT teaching about the activity of God, who "created man to rule over the world and put in him two spirits so that he might walk according to them until the time of His visitation. These are the spirits of truth and iniquity" (1QS 3:17–19). See also 1QS 3:13—4:26, which is too lengthy to be quoted here.

This dualism has already been discussed in the treatment of the theology found in QL in chap. VIII above. So only a brief summary is given here. The dualism contrasts such spirits as light and darkness, righteousness and perversity, under the dominion of the Prince of Lights or the Angel of Darkness, and describes all the effects that they have on human beings, who are divided into "sons of light/righteousness" and "sons of darkness/iniquity" (3:20–21). This dualistic system is controlled by the God of Israel, affecting human conduct but having a cosmic dimension. Hence it is at once monotheistic, ethical, and theological.

In the Johannine writings, too, such a dualism is found, along with some of the same terminology. It is expressed as a struggle between light and darkness: "The light shines in the darkness, and darkness did not overcome it" (John 1:5). It is seen also as a conflict between Jesus and the Prince of this World as they seek to influence human beings and their behavior: "Now is the judgment of this world, now shall the prince of this world be cast out; and I, when I am lifted up from the earth, will draw all human beings to myself" (John 12:31–32).

The similarity of the Essene and Johannine dualism can be found above all in the image of light and darkness, for Christians are urged to become "sons of light": "As long as you have the light, believe in the light, that you may become sons of light" (John 12:36), just as *běnê 'ôr* is used often of the members of the Essene community (1QS 1:9; 2:16; etc.).

Light and darkness, as a symbol of good and evil, occurs already in the OT (Ps 112:4; Isa 5:20), but one never finds in the OT or in the later rabbinic literature either "sons of light" or "sons of darkness," despite the fact that "sons of..." is a good Semitic expression imitating phrases like "sons of might" (Judg 18:2; 2 Kgs 2:16) or "sons of rebellion" (Num 17:25). What is distinctive, and what Bauckham and others have failed to understand, is the division of humanity into two groups using such Semitisms, "sons of light" and "sons of darkness." Such a division is encountered only in QL and in John (as well as in some other NT writings). The latter of the two phrases is admittedly not in the NT, except indirectly, by implication in the former phrase and by a similar one in "the son of destruction," used of Judas in John 17:12.

Moreover, the dualistic spirits have titles that are verbally similar: 1 John 4:6 speaks of "the spirit of truth," pitted against "the spirit of error" almost the same way "the spirits of truth and iniquity" are cast in 1QS 3:17–19 (quoted above).

The imagery of light and darkness, when ascribed to conduct or behavior, describes how human beings "walk" in light or darkness: "The one who follows me will not walk in darkness but will have the light of life" (John 8:12); "the one who walks in darkness knows not where he goes" (John 12:35); "if we say that we have companionship with Him while walking in darkness, we lie and do not practice the truth; but if we walk in the light, as He is in the light, we have companionship…" (1 John 1:6–7). Similar expressions appear in QL: "All the sons of righteousness walk on paths of light, but the sons of iniquity…walk on all the paths of darkness" (1QS 3:20–21); "to walk on all the paths of darkness" (1QS 4:11); "and I…belong to the assembly of worms and to those who walk in darkness" (1QS 11:9–10). Even "the light of life" (John 8:12) occurs in 1QS 3:7, "For through God's spirit of true counsel are expiated the paths of a human being, all his iniquities, so that he might gaze upon the light of life." To "walk in light" can mean also to "walk in the truth" (2 John 4; 3 John 3—4), which is comparable to "all who walk in it [the truth, mentioned in the preceding context]" (1QS 4:6). This association of truth and deceit/error with light and darkness shows that two of the seven pairs of Johannine opposites occur in QL too.

In John 5:33, Jesus announces that "John [the Baptist] has borne witness to the truth," and says of himself, "I have come into the world to bear witness to the truth" (John 18:37). This testimony to the truth is comparable to the Essenes, who were said to be "witnesses of truth for justice" (1QS 8:6).

The Johannine Gospel depicts Jesus praying to the Father for his disciples, "Sanctify them in the truth" (17:17). This prayer can be compared with what the Manual of Discipline says about God's activity among the Essenes, "Then God will refine with His truth all human deeds" (1QS 4:20).

Some of the last-mentioned instances are not explicitly dualistic because the counter phrase is missing; but they at least fill out the picture of the way the ideas of truth and deceit/error or light and darkness function in these writings.

3. Spirit of Truth

This title is not found in the OT, but the cosmic struggle between it and the spirit of iniquity that God has placed in human beings is described in QL:

> In the hand of the Prince of Lights is dominion over all sons of righteousness; they walk on paths of light. But in the hand of the Angel of Darkness is complete dominion over the sons of iniquity; they walk on paths of darkness. From the Angel of Darkness (also comes) the straying of all the sons of righteousness, and all their sins, their iniquities, their guilt; their offensive deeds are committed under its domination. (1QS 3:20–22).

Or again, "up until now the spirits of truth and iniquity struggle in the heart of a man" (1QS 4:23). Along with "the Prince of Lights," the "Spirit of Truth" is one of the two principles dominating the conduct of human beings in this literature.

In the Johannine writings, the formulation may not be completely the same, but the idea of the struggle is expressed: between Jesus, "the Son of God" and "the Prince of this World," that is, the devil (John 1:34; 5:25; 10:36; 12:31). "He [the Prince of this World] has no power over me [Jesus]" (John 14:30), because "he will be cast out" (John 12:31). In the Johannine writings, Jesus and the Paraclete, also called the "Spirit of Truth," are the two positive principles dominating the conduct of human beings.

4. Love of Community Members

In the Fourth Gospel, Jesus gives his most fundamental command to his followers: "A new commandment I give you: you must love one another; even as I have loved you, you too must love one another. In this shall all people know that you are my disciples, if you have love for one another" (John 13:34–35). That commandment is reformulated in 15:12; 1 John 3:11, 14; 2 John 5.

The Manual of Discipline begins with an instruction for the members of the community, which similarly stresses the love of community members: they are to "seek God with all their heart and with all their soul, so as to do what is good and upright before Him, as He commanded through Moses and all His servants the Prophets;...but also to love all the sons of light, each according to his lot in God's design" (1QS 1:2–3, 9–10). Similarly, the other rule book, the Damascus Document, instructs the Essenes that "each one must love his brother as himself" (CD 6:20; cf. 4D^d [4Q269] 4 ii 2). This love of another member of the community is explained further by the instruction that "one should reprove his fellow-member in truth, in meekness, and compassionate love for each one" (1QS 5:25–26). "Sons of light" are members of the Essene community.

The love of "the sons of light" has a counterpart in QL in the hatred of "the sons of darkness" (1QS 1:10–11), but such hatred is not found in Jesus' teaching recorded in the Johannine writings, even though the evangelist depicts Jesus purging the Temple of those who were defiling His Father's house (John 2:11–17).

5. Other Miscellaneous Parallels

The parallels that will be presented here are not dualistic pairs such as light and darkness, but are a different sort that may be equally important as the pairs.

(a) In John 1:19–23, shortly after the end of the prologue, the evangelist devotes these verses to the testimony of John the Baptist, who answers the questions of those sent by Jerusalem authorities who wanted to know who he was. He answered, "I am not the Messiah," and not "Elijah" and not "the prophet." Instead he admitted that he was "the voice of someone crying in the wilderness: make straight the way of the Lord, as Isaiah the prophet said." The questions asked of John reveal the vivid expectation that Palestinian Jews of that time had about the coming of three figures: Elijah, who was promised in Mal 3:23; a prophet, that is, the prophet like Moses, promised in Deut 18:15, 18; and an Anointed One, promised in Dan 9:25, where *māšîaḥ* appears for the first time in the OT in the sense of an *expected* Anointed One (or Messiah). John insisted that he was not one of these figures.

These verses in the Johannine Gospel are thus important as an echo of the Essene expectation of three coming figures: "a prophet and the Messiahs of Aaron and Israel" (1QS 9:10–11).[6] Elijah, who is mentioned in John's Gospel, is not one of the three expected by the Essenes, who rather awaited the coming of two Messiahs, one priestly and one kingly (of the Davidic dynasty). This may have been a conviction peculiar to the Essenes, for no one knows whether other Jews awaited the same number of Messiahs.

(b) The notion of "eternal life" (*ḥayyê 'ôlām*) occurs in Dan 12:2 as the reward of "the wise," but it is a concept that appears often in the Johannine writings (e.g., John 3:15–16, 36; 4:14; 10:28; 1 John 1:2; 2:25) as the destiny of believers. Similarly, it is found in QL, where it is promised as "a reward for all who walk in it [i.e., in the spirit of light/truth]: healing, abundance of peace in length of days, fruitful seed with endless blessings, everlasting joy in life eternal (*ḥayyê nēṣaḥ*) and a glorious crown with majestic raiment in eternal light" (1QS 4:6–8). Or again, "Those who cling steadfastly to it [i.e., to the same house in Israel] are (destined) for eternal life (*lĕḥayyê nēṣaḥ*), and all the glory of Adam will be theirs" (CD 3:20).

(c) "Living water" (*hydōr zōn*) of which Jesus speaks is unique to the Fourth Gospel, for it never appears on his lips in the Synoptic Gospels. Jesus mentions it in his conversation with the Samaritan woman (John 4:10–11), and when he invites the one who would believe in him to come to him and drink, as Scripture says, "Out of his innards shall flow rivers of living water" (paraphrasing Zech 14:8 in John 7:39). In the QL, the author of the Thanksgiving Psalms sings of the favors received from God and employs the same phrase, "But You, my God, have put in my mouth, as it were, an early rain for all [. . . . .] and a spring of living water" (1QHᵃ 16 [old 8]:16). Likewise, "a source of living water" is mentioned, but the context is lacking because of the fragmentary state of the text (4QDibHamᵃ [4Q504] 1–2 v 1).

(d) "The works of God" (*ta erga tou theou*) is a phrase that a crowd of people use, when they ask Jesus how they must conduct themselves to do "the works of God," and Jesus answers, "This is the work of God (*to ergon tou theou*) that you believe in him whom

He has sent" (John 6:28–29). For a long time, commentators on John's Gospel have debated the meaning of "the works of God."[7] But the meaning is clarified by CD 2:14–15: "And now, children, listen to me; I shall open your eyes to see and understand the works of God, so that you may choose what is pleasing to Him and reject what He hates, so as to walk perfectly." The goal of doing what God desires is different in the two writings: faith in John and proper choice in CD, but in both instances the phrase "works of God" denotes what God demands of human beings.

(e) Idols. 1 John 5:21, with which the epistle ends, warns, "Little children, stay away from idols." Similarly, the Essenes of Qumran were admonished, "Cursed be the one who enters this covenant with the idols that his heart reveres" (1QS 2:11–12). Likewise the Damascus Document depicts those members of the community who are slack in the observance of its regulations as having "placed idols (*gillûlîm*) in their hearts" (CD 20:9). See also 1QH 12 [old 4]:15.

All these features and parallels, which differ in their similarity, reveal that the Johannine writings owe much to a Palestinian Jewish background. The verbal and conceptual parallels in the Johannine writings manifest a real contact with QL, even though it is only indirect, that is, via some person(s) whom one can identify only by speculation—perhaps, as R. E. Brown once proposed, through the disciples of John the Baptist, who are mentioned in John 1:35, 37; 3:25. Such parallels, however, have not "revolutionized our understanding of the Gospel of John," as has been claimed at times.[8] For the contemporary interpretation of the Johannine Gospel owes much to many factors other than the Qumran writings, important though the latter may be for that understanding.

XII

THE SCROLLS AND OTHER CHRISTIAN WRITINGS

Now that the discussion of the impact of the Dead Sea Scrolls on the Pauline and Johannine writings is complete, I have to turn to the Synoptic Gospels and other NT writings such as the Epistle to the Hebrews and the Apocalypse.

1. The Synoptic Gospels

There are a number of features in the Synoptic Gospels the interpretation of which has profited from comparison with similar items in the Qumran Scrolls. For instance:

(a) The Beatitudes. A beatitude or macarism is a saying that begins, "Blessed is/are….The beatitude as a literary form is found often in the OT (e.g., Ps 1:1; Jer 17:7); sometimes beatitudes are paired (e.g., Ps 32:1–2). There are thirteen beatitudes in the Matthean Gospel, and fifteen in the Lucan. They appear on the lips of Jesus, scattered throughout his teaching. A collection of beatitudes is found in Matt 5:3–10 (eight of them) and in Luke 6:20–22 (four of them, parallel to four woes).

Beatitudes are scattered throughout QL, especially in its Wisdom texts. Thus, "Blessed is the man to whom she [Wisdom] has been given" (4QWisText [4Q185] 1–2 ii 8); "Blessed is the man who makes(?) her [Wisdom], does not deceive her, does not slander against her…" (ibid., 13).

A collection of beatitudes is found in 4QBeat (4Q525) 2 ii 1–7, which reads:

[Blessed is the one who speaks truth] with pure heart and slanders not with his tongue. Blessed are those who cling to her statutes and cling not to paths of iniquity. Blessed are those who rejoice in her and babble not about paths of iniquity. Blessed are those who search for her with clean hands and seek not after her with a deceitful heart. Blessed is the man who has attained Wisdom, walks in the law of the Most High, fixes his heart on her ways, gives heed to her admonishments, and delights always in her chastisements, and forsakes her not in the stress of his troubles; who in time of distress abandons her not and forgets her not in days of fear, and in the affliction of his soul rejects her not. For on her he meditates, and in his anguish he ponders on the law, and in all his existence he considers her and puts her before his eyes so as not to walk in the paths of [   ]

In this sapiential writing, there are five beatitudes. The feminine pronoun refers to Wisdom, a feminine noun (*ḥokmāh*), mentioned in line 7 above; but it could refer conceivably to "the law of the Most High" (*tôrat ʿelyôn*), which also is feminine. It does not matter, because "the law of the Most High" is "Wisdom." This collection of beatitudes, then, shows that such a literary form was already in vogue in Palestinian Judaism and that the evangelists imitated it. There is a difference, however, because the Qumran beatitudes dwell on one topic, Wisdom, and its influence on human conduct, whereas Jesus' beatitudes not only are sapiential and concerned with human conduct, but are also eschatological.[1]

(b) Prohibition of Divorce. The prohibition of divorce by Jesus is found in several places in the NT. Its earliest attestation occurs in 1 Cor 7:10–11, where Paul repeats it in indirect discourse: "To the married I give this command, not I but the Lord: that a wife should not be separated from her husband; but if indeed she is separated, she must either remain unmarried or be reconciled to her husband; and that a husband should not divorce his wife." The most primitive form, however, is recorded by Luke, "Anyone who divorces his wife and marries another woman commits adultery; and anyone who marries a woman divorced from her husband commits adultery" (16:18). This form is regarded as the most primitive because, of all the forms preserved, it is the one that corresponds best to the Palestinian Jewish understanding of the relation of a woman to a man in marriage at the time of Jesus. In that understanding, the woman married to a man was considered his property or chattel (implied in Exod 20:17b; 21:3, 22; Jer 6:12; Num 30:10–14; Esth 1:20–22; Sir 23:22–27). To divorce a wife was permitted to a man (Deut 24:1–4: "a writ of divorce"), but a woman could not divorce her husband.

The Essene attitude to divorce is found in 11QTemple[a] (11Q19) 57:17–19, "He [the king] shall take no other wife in addition to her, for she alone will be with him all the days of her life; and if she dies, he shall take for himself another (woman) from his father's house, from his family." At first, these words may sound like a prohibition of polygamy, but when one understands the meaning of "she alone (*hî'āh lĕbaddāh*)...all the days of her life," one sees clearly that the words refer to polygamy and divorce. The prohibition of divorce in this 11Q text concerns explicitly the king, but what is legislated for the king is legislated also for the commoner. Some commentators think that CD 4:20—5:2, which forbids the taking of "two wives in their lifetime," is a prohibition of divorce; but that text is far from clear.

In any case, the 11Q19 text clearly does prohibit divorce and provides the Palestinian Jewish background for Jesus' own prohibition. So when the Pharisees ask Jesus in Mark 10:2, "Is it lawful for a man to divorce his wife?" his answer to them is, in effect, that he agrees with the Essenes, who undoubtedly based their view of it on Mal 2:16a: "'I hate divorce,' says the Lord God of Israel."

(c) The Baptist's Question. In Luke 7:19–23, the evangelist tells of John the Baptist sending messengers to Jesus to ask him, "Are you the 'One who is to come,' or are we to look for someone else?" The evangelist gives them an answer by recounting how Jesus has cured many people and restored sight to the blind, and by having Jesus say, "Go and inform John of what you have seen and heard: Blind recovering their sight, cripples walking, lepers being cleansed, deaf hearing again, dead being raised to life, and good news preached to the poor." Jesus' answer uses phrases drawn from OT passages such as Isa 35:5; 26:19.

Jesus' answer also sounds very much like an important apocalyptic text, 4QApocMess (4Q521) 2 ii 1–14, which reads:

[For the hea]vens and the earth will listen to His Messiah, and all that is in them will not swerve from the commandments of the holy ones. Be strengthened in His service, all you who seek the Lord! [Blank] Shall you not find the Lord in this, all those [= you] who hope in their hearts? For the Lord shall seek out the pious, and the righteous He shall call by name. Over afflicted ones shall His Spirit hover, and faithful ones He shall renew with His power. He shall honor the pious on a throne of eternal kingship, freeing prisoners, giving sight to the blind, straightening up those bent over. "Forever will I cling to those who hope, and with His steadfast love He shall recompense: the fruit of a good deed shall be delayed for no one." Wondrous things, such as have never been before, will the Lord do, just as He said. For He shall heal the wounded, revive the dead, and proclaim good news to the afflicted; the poor He shall satiate, the uprooted He shall guide, and on the hungry He shall bestow riches; as for the intelligent, all of them shall be like holy ones.

The wording of this passage is heavily dependent on Psalm 146, which lauds God for the help He has provided to the downtrodden in view of their eschatological salvation. The wording, however, is considerably modified, especially by the introduction of "His Messiah," which does not appear in Psalm 146. As the passage is interpreted sometimes, the wondrous deeds are ascribed to the Messiah; but line 4 ends with a blank, and the subject of lines 6 through the end is "the Lord." So the wondrous deeds are the Lord's, which He will accomplish in the days of His Messiah.

In any case, this Messianic Apocalypse from Qumran Cave 4 supplies an interesting parallel to Jesus' answer to the messengers of John the Baptist.

(d) Son of God. In Luke 1:32–35, the angel Gabriel announces to Mary that the child to be born of her will be "great" and will be called "Son of the Most High" and "Son of God." This announcement and these titles have a remarkable parallel in 4QSon of God (4Q246), which has already been discussed earlier (see p. 66 above).

2. The Epistle to the Hebrews

The NT writing that is so named is recognized today as neither a Pauline composition, nor an epistle, nor addressed to the Hebrews, despite the long tradition that so regarded it. It is an anonymous homily or word of exhortation (*logos paraklēseōs*, so named in Heb 13:22) with an epistolary conclusion, addressed to a Christian community and seeking to get it to renew its loyalty after considerable backsliding. It contains extensive exhortations, with elaborate interpretations of OT passages.

The Jewish scholar Y. Yadin, in an early article written in 1958, maintained that the Epistle to the Hebrews was addressed to a "group of Jews originally belonging to the DSS Sect who were converted to Christianity, carrying with them some of their previous beliefs."[2] His opinion was adopted by some Christian scholars.

(a) Jesus' Role in Hebrews

Jesus is depicted not only as superior to the prophets, angels, and Moses but also as a priest (*hiereus*) or high priest (*archiereus*). This title is given to him only in this epistle, and nowhere else in the NT. Jesus is, then, a priestly Messiah, but of an order superior to that of Aaron: "…we have a great high priest who has passed through the heavens, Jesus, the Son of God,…designated by God a high priest according to the order of Melchizedek" (4:14; 5:10; see also 5:5–6). This is an allusion to Gen 14:18–20 and Ps 110:4, but to appreciate the full meaning of these allusions, it is necessary to learn how these passages were understood in Palestinian Judaism in the last pre-Christian centuries. This is where the tradition about Melchizedek in QL makes a valuable contribution.

(i) Melchizedek in the OT. The name Melchizedek is *Malkî-ṣedeq* in Hebrew, meaning "Ṣedeq is my king"—Ṣedeq being the name of a Canaanite god. It is said to mean, however, "king of righteousness" (Heb 7:2) or "righteous king" (*basileus dikaios*, Josephus, *Ant.* 1.10.2 §180; Philo, *Legum allegoriae* 3 §79). This explanation of the Canaanite name shows how it was "judaized" and then imitated by Christians.

Melchizedek appears first in Genesis 14, in verses that follow the account of Abram's defeat of the invading kings:

> Melchizedek, king of Salem, brought out bread and wine; he was a priest of God Most High. He blessed him, saying, "Blest be Abram by God Most High, maker of heaven and earth, and blest be God Most High, who has delivered your enemies into your hand!" And he gave him a tenth of everything. (Gen 14:18–20)

Melchizedek is mentioned further in the OT only in the royal psalm that promises victory to some king of the Davidic dynasty. Ps 110:4 reads, "You are a priest forever according to the order of Melchizedek." This cryptic allusion refers to the passage of Genesis 14 just quoted.

The three verses in Genesis 14 interrupt the story of the king of Sodom, which began in 14:17 and is continued in 14:21. Many commentators consider these verses to be an independent account introduced secondarily into chap. 14. Moreover, the mention of Melchizedek as a "priest of God Most High" creates a difficulty: How could anyone be called a priest of God Most High whose genealogy was not known? All of this has to be attributed to the fact that the Melchizedek verses were originally an independent description of him as a priest of a Canaanite god called El Elyon. When the verses were adopted and inserted into the Hebrew story of the king of Sodom, they took on a Jewish, monotheistic meaning. El Elyon became a title of the God of the Israelites, and so Melchizedek became a priest of God Most High, even though his genealogy was unknown.

(ii) Melchizedek in QL. Genesis 14:18–20, however, is retold in an embellished account in an Aramaic translation that reads:

> Melchizedek, the king of Salem, brought out food and drink for Abram and for all the men who were with him. He was a priest of God Most High, and he blessed Abram and said, "Blest be Abram by God Most High, Lord of heaven and earth! Blest be God Most High, who has delivered your enemies into your hand." And he gave him a tithe from all the goods of the King of Elam and his confederates. (1QapGen [1Q20] 22:14–17)[3]

This version of the Melchizedek story clarifies a number of items that were not clear in the Genesis account. "Food and drink" makes it clear that the "bread and wine" of Gen 14:18 were meant as refreshment for the returning warriors, as Josephus also understood it (*Ant.* 1.10.2 §181). In Gen 14:20, it is not clear who gave the "tenth of everything" to whom. However, just as in Heb 7:2, so too here no doubt is left: Abram pays the tithe to Melchizedek. In Heb 7:2, the author inserted the name *Abraam* as the subject. This version also specifies that the tithe came not from "everything" (Gen 14:20) but "from all the goods of the King of Elam and his confederates."

Melchizedek is mentioned in another text from Qumran Cave 11, called 11QMelch (11Q13) 2:7–16, which reads:

> The Day of Atonement is the end of the tenth jubilee, in which expiation shall be made for all the sons of light and for the men of the lot of Melchizedek, according to all their deeds. For it is the time for the year of grace for Melchizedek and for his armies, the nation of the holy ones of God....As for the rule of justice, there is written about it in the Songs of David, who said, "Elohim has stood in the divine council; in the midst of the gods he judges" [Ps 82:1].
>
> About him it says, "Over it, on high, return: God will judge the peoples" [Ps 7:8–9]. As for what it says, "How long will you judge unjustly and show partiality to the wicked? *Selah*" [Ps 82:2]. The meaning of it concerns Belial and the spirits of his lot, who were turning aside from the commandments of God to commit evil. But

> Melchizedek shall carry out the vengeance of God's judgments; and on that day he shall free them from the hand of Belial and from the hands of all the spirits of his lot. To his aid shall come all "the gods of justice"; and he is the one who[ ] all the sons of God. This is the day of peace about which he spoke through the prophet Isaiah, "How beautiful upon the mountains are the feet of the messenger who announces peace, the messenger of good who announces salvation, saying to Zion, Your God reigns" [Isa 52:7].

This text portrays Melchizedek no longer as an earthly priest-king, but as a heavenly being among the gods (i.e., angels) in heaven during a jubilee year (cf. Lev 25:8–24), when on the Day of Atonement Melchizedek is to make expiation for all those who belong to his lot.

(iii) Melchizedek in the Epistle to the Hebrews. In Heb 7:3, after Melchizedek's name has been translated and interpreted, the author comments that "he is without father or mother or genealogy," which sounds very strange. Yet if one recalls what was explained above about the secondary and independent character of Gen 14:18–20 and their insertion into chap. 14, one can understand how the author can make that comment. In those verses Melchizedek has no father or mother or genealogy.

In that same verse (Heb 7:3), the author continues, "He has neither beginning of days nor end of life, but resembling the Son of God he continues as a priest forever." The text of 11QMelch (11Q13) portrays the exaltation of Melchizedek as a heavenly figure of redemption. This would enable the author of Hebrews to argue for the superiority of Christ the High Priest over the levitical priests of old, because "resembling the Son of God, he continues as a priest forever," and does not depend on descent from priestly generations. He is like the heavenly Melchizedek.

3. The Book of Revelation

This distinctive book of the NT is called properly by the Greek title, "The Apocalypse" (*Apokalypsis*), because it is the only complete book in the NT written in the literary genre called "apocalyptic." This genre designates writings of a revelatory character that were born in ancient Judaism, especially in times when Israel was struggling with occupying powers that were persecuting the Israelites. The purpose of such a writing was to console the Israelites, assuring them that God was still in control of their destiny and history. Examples of such apocalyptic writing can be found in Isaiah 24—27, 56—66; Zechariah 9—14; Daniel 7—12; and in noncanonical Jewish literature such as *Jubilees, 1 Enoch,* and *4 Ezra.*

The Apocalypse is distinctive in its use of "stage-props," such as visions, dreams, cosmic battles, seals, trumpets, bowls, numbers, colors, cryptic names, angels, demons, beasts, all blended in with numerous historical allusions and code names (e.g., for Roman emperors). Many of these features have an OT background.

The Apocalypse begins with an epistolary prologue and an introductory vision (chap. 1); then follow the Letters to Seven Churches (chaps. 2—3); an inaugural vision of God's glory and the Savior Lamb (chaps. 4—5); a vision of heaven's move against Israel (chaps. 6—11); a vision of heaven's move against pagan Rome (chaps. 12—20); a vision of the New Jerusalem as the refuge of God's people (21:1—22:7); and an epistolary conclusion (22:8-21).

In QL, some apocalyptic writings have been found, but none resembling the Apocalypse of the NT; nor is there any writing completely of that genre. The closest work is the War Scroll from Qumran Cave 1 (1QM [sometimes called 1Q33]; also a copy from Cave 4, 4QM), but it is really a rule book, bearing the title, *serek hammilhāmāh,* "Rule of the War."[4] Yet it is rife with what has been called apocalyptic eschatology in its description of the war of the end-time. It has, moreover, many apocalyptic "stage-props": trumpets (2:16—3:10), banners (3:13—4:17), symbolic language, code names (e.g., 1:12; 15:2, Kittim [= Romans]).

Other, less pronounced apocalyptic writings are 4QSon of God (4Q246); New Jerusalem texts (1QNJ [1Q32], 2QNJ [2Q24], 4QNJ [4Q232], 5QNJ [5Q15], 11QNJ [11Q18]); 4QFour Kgdms[a-b] (4Q552–553); 4QShirShabb[d] (4Q403). From these writings, one finds the best parallels in the New Jerusalem texts, of which 5Q15 is the most extensive. In these NJ texts, a seer is led around the city by an unnamed guide, who uses a measuring rod with which he measures the walls of the square city: "He also showed me the dimensions of all the blocks. Between one block and another was the street, six rods wide, forty-two cubits. The main streets run from east to west; the width of the street was ten rods, seventy cubits; and the street that passes to the left of the Temple he measured (as) eighteen rods, 126 cubits..." (5Q15 1 i 2–4). Such a description illustrates the measuring of the New Jerusalem in Rev 21:15–17.

In Rev 21:12–13 one reads, "It [Jerusalem] had a big, high wall, with twelve gates, and at the gates twelve angels, and on the gates the names of the twelve tribes of the children of Israel were inscribed, on the east three gates, on the north three gates, on the south three gates, and on the west three gates." Compare 11QTemple[a] 39:11–13: "The names of the gates of this court are according to the names of the children of Israel: Simeon, Levi, and Judah to the east; Reuben, Joseph, and Benjamin to the south; Issachar, Zebulun, and Gad to the west; Dan, Naphtali, and Asher to the north." The details are not all identical, but the thrust of the two passages certainly is; and both of these writings, in their description of the New Jerusalem, depend on Ezekiel 40—48.

The walls of the New Jerusalem "were adorned with every jewel:...jasper,...sapphire,...agate,...emerald,...onyx,...carnelian, ...chrysolite,...beryl,...topaz,...chrysoprase,...jacinth,...amethyst" (Rev 21:19–20). Compare 4QNJ[a] (4Q554) 2 ii 14–15: "And it [the city's foundation] is built entirely of electrum and sapphire, and of chalcedony; and its laths are of gold...."

The New Jerusalem of Revelation 21 has no Temple, because the Lord God and the Lamb are the Temple. So all the emphasis is put on "the city," which needs no sun or moon and the gates of which "shall never be shut" (21:22–25). "But nothing unclean shall enter it, nor anyone who practices abomination or falsehood" (21:27). This prohibition finds a parallel in similar impurities prohibited from the Temple in 11QTemple[a] 45:7–12: "The man who has had a nocturnal emission shall not enter any of the temple until three days have passed," and he has bathed. Or "anyone who is impure because of contact with a corpse shall not enter it until he has purified himself; nor any leper or infected person..." (45:17–18).

There is a peculiar saying in Rev 9:13, when the sixth angel blows his trumpet: "I heard a voice from the four horns of the golden altar before God, saying to the sixth angel...." Commentators have debated whether it was the voice of an angel or of God; but it may be the voice of the personified four horns of the altar, as in 4QShirShabb[d] (4Q403) 1 i 41–42: "With them [i.e., with the angels, called the Holy Ones] shall praise all the foundations of the Holy of Holies, the supporting pillars of the exalted dwelling, and all the corners of His building. Sing to God...most pure vault of His sanctuary...." Again, the author of the Apocalypse in the letter to the angel of the church in Philadelphia speaks of a living pillar, "I will make him [the one who conquers] a pillar in the temple of my God; never shall he go out of it" (Rev 3:12). That resembles the personified "supporting pillars" that sing praise in the same Qumran text.

XIII

THE COPPER SCROLL

In Qumran Cave 3, the archaeologists who were scouring the cliffs that line the northwest shore of the Dead Sea in the spring of 1952 as they looked for further caves after the discovery of Cave 2 found a strange object. It turned out to be two copper rolls, each about 12 inches long, which had lain in the cave for about 2,000 years. The copper rolls could not be unrolled because the metal had become oxidized and brittle. They have often been called "the Copper Scroll," the title used in this chapter. They are not really a scroll, but rather two parts of a plaque. It soon became clear that the plaque contained some writing, because some of the letters of the inscribed text showed through on the reverse. A German scholar, Karl Georg Kuhn, who studied the unrolled plaque, determined from the inverse letters that the text had something to do with "digging," "cubits," and "gold." From this he concluded that it probably said something about hidden treasure.

After several attempts were made to unroll the plaque, John Marco Allegro, a member of the international team that was working on the fragments of Qumran Cave 4 in the Palestine Archaeological Museum in Jerusalem, was permitted in 1955 to take the plaque to Manchester in England. There H. Wright Baker, a professor of mechanical engineering in the Manchester College of Science and Technology, devised a way to cut the plaque into vertical columns, which were discernible on the reverse, with a saw that was used usually to split pen nibs. So the two parts of the plaque were opened finally, and the inscribed text could be read: 23 columns of Hebrew letters on the concave copper strips.

Allegro made a facsimile of the Hebrew letters to accompany the photographs of the columns; the photographs were difficult to read because of the curvature of the strips, and so the facsimile

Copper Scrolls (3Q15) found in 1952 in Cave 3

became all important. Allegro finally brought the facsimile, the photographs, and unrolled plaque back to Jerusalem. Then J. T. Milik was assigned to make the official publication of it, which he finally did in 1962, seven years after it was opened.[1]

Because Milik had taken so long with the official publication, Allegro satisfied the eagerness of the general public for information about the plaque with his own study of it, *The Treasure of the Copper Scroll: The Opening and Decipherment of the Most Mysterious of the Dead Sea Scrolls, a Unique Inventory of Buried Treasure.*[2]

When the text of 3Q15 was studied, it revealed that it was indeed a list of 64 places were treasure had been buried, as Kuhn had suggested from his study of it in its unopened state. For instance, the first entry of column 1 reads, "At Harubah, which is in the Vale of Achor, under the steps that face eastward, 40 cubits: a box of silver weighing 17 talents. KεN." In this entry, the details are somewhat clear, but in many of the 64 entries they are not. The Hebrew text of the first entry just quoted ends with three Greek letters, and nobody has been able to say what they (and a few other instances like them) really mean. What is evident, however, is that the whole text records the hiding places of many precious metals: gold, silver, and other items.

Again, the fifty-seventh entry of 3Q15 reads, "At Betheshdatayin in the pool, where you enter its small reservoir, vessels of...." The name "Betheshdatayin" means literally "the house of the two gushers." According to J. Jeremias, this is a reference to Bethesda, which was a variant reading of the name "Bethzatha" in John 5:2: "Now there was in Jerusalem...a pool, called in Hebrew Bethesda, which has five porticoes." These words describe a rectangular reservoir divided in half by a middle portico, which thus numbered five porticoes and created two pools, into which the water gushed intermittently, so that the infirm could go into either of the pools.[3] The location in the fifty-seventh entry of 3Q15 seems to be describing this five-porticoed reservoir, making clear that one pool was smaller than the other. Thus, the contents of this list of 64 locations where treasures had been buried reveal its importance.

The opened plaque, however, has raised many questions. Does it record places where real treasure has been buried? Was it the treasure of the Qumran community? Or did the treasure belong to someone else? Possibly to the Temple in Jerusalem? Who stored the plaque in Cave 3? Or was it merely a fictional record of "buried treasure"? There are other ancient examples of imaginary buried treasure, but none on a copper plaque. But if it is a fictional record, why would anyone inscribe it on a copper plaque?

Whatever the answers to such questions may be, the text inscribed on the plaque is important for the study of the Hebrew dialect in which it was composed. It is written in a form of Hebrew that is intermediate between the late postexilic Biblical Hebrew (and even Qumran Hebrew) and Mishnaic Hebrew. Milik dated the script palaeographically to A.D. 100. If he is correct, that would mean that the plaque was deposited in Cave 3 after the destruction of the Essene community center at Qumran in A.D. 68 and the destruction of Jerusalem in A.D. 70. It is far from certain that the plaque had anything to do with the Essene community, because its text contains no sectarian terminology and mentions no one or anything connected with the Essenes.

Allegro believed that the text told of real buried treasure and mounted expeditions to go in search of it in the various locations that he thought he could identify, but he was not able to find anything, despite the support that he had from various institutions, including the king of Jordan.

Today, the majority of scholars who have been studying the text of this plaque are convinced that it records the treasure of the Temple, which Jerusalem authorities buried before the Romans captured and destroyed the city.[4]

XIV

THE END OF THE QUMRAN COMMUNITY

From the archaeological evidence at Khirbet Qumran, it is known that the site was destroyed by fire, and in the ashes created by it were found coins dated to the second and third year of the First Jewish Revolt against Rome, along with numerous arrowheads.[1] This means that the buildings were destroyed by military action, that is, by the Roman troops that were in the Jordan Valley prior to their advance to the siege of Jerusalem. Hence, the site of Qumran became ruins (a *khirbeh*) in A.D. 68, and the Essenes had to move on from there. The Romans left a small squadron of soldiers at Qumran, who used part of the site as military post to guard the shore of the Dead Sea and the area around the mouth of the Jordan River.

Some of the Essenes from Qumran must have gone to Masada, a Herodian fortress situated about 25 miles to the south-southwest of Qumran, because copies of some of the same texts that were found in Qumran Cave 4 were also found there, written in the same script. The fortress of Masada fell to the Roman siege of it in A.D. 73–74, and what Essenes from Qumran were there must have either perished or fled elsewhere.

In the Acts of the Apostles, Luke wrote in one of his summary statements that "the word of God continued to spread, and the number of disciples in Jerusalem greatly increased; a large number of priests became obedient to the faith" (6:7). Were some of the priests of the Essenes of Qumran among such converts? We know that there had been Essenes in Jerusalem too. No one, however, can answer that question, even if it remains possible.

ARCHAEOLOGICAL SITE OF COMMUNITY ROOM AT QUMRAN

Since the phrase *'ădat hā'ebyônîm*, "congregation of the poor," occurs in some Qumran texts as a title for the Qumran community (4QpPs^a [4Q171] 1–2 ii 9; 1, 3–4 iii 10), remnants of the community may have become Christians and were eventually known as "Ebionites." About such Jewish Christians we learn in writings of the patristic period (Justin Martyr, Irenaeus, Origen, Eusebius). In fact, in the early days of the debate about the identity of the Qumran community, some scholars (J. L. Teicher, H.-J. Schoeps) wanted to call it Ebionite instead of Essene. That was hardly likely, however, because the Qumran community was Jewish, not Christian. Yet it still remains possible that some former members of that group became Ebionites after the destruction of Qumran.

It is not impossible that some of the Qumran community became Christian monks, because from the Manual of Discipline and other sectarian writings we know that the Essenes lived a common life, pooled their earnings, and conducted themselves in obedience to an Overseer (*mĕbaqqēr*); and some of them lived as celibates. That form of life was thus a Jewish precedent of the life of poverty, chastity, and obedience that characterized monasticism in the Christian church of later days.

NOTES

I. The Dead Sea Scrolls: Terminology, Discovery, and Dating

1. See M. Burrows et al. (eds.), *The Dead Sea Scrolls of St Mark's Monastery*, vol. 1, *The Isaiah Manuscript and Habakkuk Commentary* (New Haven, CT: American Schools of Oriental Research, 1950).

2. See M. Burrows et al. (eds.), *The Dead Sea Scrolls of St Mark's Monastery*, vol. 2, fascicle 2, *Plates and Transcription of the Manual of Discipline* (New Haven, CT: American Schools of Oriental Research, 1951).

3. See E. L. Sukenik, *'Oṣar hmgylwt hgnwzwt* (2 parts; Jerusalem: Bialik Institute and Hebrew University, 1954).

4. See N. Avigad and Y. Yadin, *A Genesis Apocryphon: A Scroll from the Wilderness of Judaea* (Jerusalem: Magnes Press of the Hebrew University and Shrine of the Book, 1956).

5. See S. Zeitlin, "Scholarship and the Hoax of Recent Discoveries," *JQR* 39 (1947–48): 337–63. Cf. W. F. Albright, "Are the 'Ain Feshkha Scrolls a Hoax?" *JQR* 40 (1949–50): 41–49.

6. See J. L. Teicher, "The Dead Sea Scrolls—Documents of the Jewish-Christian Sect of the Ebionites," *JJS* 2 (1951): 67–99. Cf. J. A. Fitzmyer, "The Qumran Scrolls, the Ebionites, and Their Literature," *TS* 16 (1955): 335–72; reprinted in slightly abridged form in *The Scrolls and the New Testament* (ed. K. Stendahl; New York: Harper & Row, 1957), 208–31. This book has been reprinted under the same title, but with a new introduction by J. H. Charlesworth (New York: Crossroad, 1992).

7. See C. Roth, "Dead Sea Scrolls Attributed to Zealots: A New Perspective," *Manchester Guardian* 24/5 (1957): 60–72. A similar explanation of the scrolls had been proposed earlier by the Oxford University professor G. R. Driver, *The Hebrew Scrolls from*

the Neighbourhood of Jericho and the Dead Sea (London: Oxford University Press, 1951).

8. See F. M. Cross, "The Development of Jewish Scripts," in *The Bible and the Ancient Near East: Essays in Honor of William Foxwell Albright* (ed. G. E. Wright; Winona Lake, IN: Eisenbrauns, 1979), 131–203; idem, "Palaeography and the Dead Sea Scrolls," in *The Dead Sea Scrolls after Fifty Years: A Comprehensive Assessment* (2 vols.; ed. P. W. Flint and J. C. VanderKam; Leiden: Brill, 1998), 1:379–402.

9. See G. Bonani et al., "Radiocarbon Dating of the Dead Sea Scrolls," *'Atiqot* 20 (1991): 27–32; idem, "Radiocarbon Dating of Fourteen Dead Sea Scrolls," *Radiocarbon* 34 (1992): 843–49; also A. J. T. Jull et al., "Radiocarbon Dating of Scrolls and Linen Fragments from the Judean Desert," *'Atiqot* 28 (1996): 85–91; also in *Radiocarbon* 37 (1995): 11–19. Cf. H. S[hanks], "Carbon-14 Tests Substantiate Scroll Dates," *BARev* 17/6 (1991): 72.

II. The Dead Sea Scrolls: Archaeology, the Excavation of Khirbet Qumran

1. See R. de Vaux, *L'Archéologie et les manuscrits de la Mer Morte* (London: Oxford University Press for the British Academy, 1961); and in a revised form, *Archaeology and the Dead Sea Scrolls* (1973). Cf. J. Magness, "Qumran: The Site of the Dead Sea Scrolls: A Review Article," *RevQ* 22 (2005–6): 641–64.

2. See B. Schultz, "The Qumran Cemetery: 150 Years of Research," *DSD* 13 (2006): 194–228; J. E. Taylor, "The Cemeteries of Khirbet Qumran and Women's Presence at the Site," *DSD* 6 (1999): 285–323.

3. See J.-B. Humbert and A. Chambon (eds.), *Fouilles de Khirbet Qumrân et de Aïn Feshkha*, vol. 1, *Album de photographies. Répertoire du fonds photographique. Synthèse des notes de chantier du Père Roland de Vaux*, OP (NTOA, Series Archaeologica 1; Fribourg, Suisse: Éditions Universitaires; Göttingen: Vandenhoeck & Ruprecht, 1994); vol. 1B, *The Excavations of Khirbet Qumran and Ain Feshkha: Synthesis of Roland de Vaux's Field Notes* (NTOA, Series Archaeologica 1B; trans. S. J. Pfann; Fribourg: University Press;

Göttingen: Vandenhoeck & Ruprecht, 2003). Cf. J.-B. Humbert and J. Gunneweg (eds.), *Khirbet Qumrân et ʿAin Feshkha II: Études d'anthropologie, de physique et de chimie. Studies of Anthropology, Physics and Chemistry* (NTOA, Series Archaeologica 3; Fribourg: Academic Press; Göttingen: Vandenhoeck & Ruprecht, 2003). It is not certain that these works represent all of the Final Report.

4. See E.-M. Laperrousaz, *Qoumrân: L'Établissement essénien des bord de la Mer Morte: Histoire et archéologie du site* (Paris: A. & J. Picard, 1976).

5. See R. Donceel and P. Donceel-Voûte, "The Archaeology of Khirbet Qumran," in *Methods of Investigation of the Dead Sea Scrolls and the Khirbet Qumran Site: Present Realities and Future Prospects* (Annals of the New York Academy of Sciences 722; ed. M. O. Wise et al.; New York: New York Academy of Sciences, 1994), 1–38; R. Donceel, "Qumran," *The Oxford Encyclopedia of Archaeology in the Near East* (5 vols.; ed. E. M. Meyers; New York: Oxford University Press, 1997), 4:392–96. Cf. *Archaeologia* 298 (1994): 24–35. Cf. J. Magness, "A Villa at Khirbet Qumran?" *RevQ* 16 (1993–95): 397–419.

6. See N. Golb, *Who Wrote the Dead Sea Scrolls?* (New York: Simon & Shuster, 1995), 3–41.

7. See Y. Hirschfeld, *Qumran in Context: Reassessing the Archaeological Evidence* (Peabody, MA: Hendrickson, 2004).

8. See J. Magness, *The Archaeology of Qumran and the Dead Sea Scrolls* (Grand Rapids: Eerdmans, 2002).

III. The Palestinian Jewish Sect of the Essenes: History and Organization

1. Josephus supplies further information on Essenes in *J.W.* 2.20.4 §567; 3.2.1 §11; 5.4.2 §145; *Ant.* 13.5.9 §§171–73; 15.10.4 §§371–79; 18.1.2–5 §§11–22; *Life* 2 §§10–12.

2. E.g., in the Loeb Classical Library, *Josephus* (9 vols.; repr. Cambridge, MA: Harvard University Press, 1967), 2:369–87.

3. See the Loeb Classical Library, *Philo* (10 vols.; Cambridge, MA: Harvard University Press, 1967), 9:53–63, 119, 437–43.

4. All these sources (and a few others of lesser importance) can be found conveniently gathered in G. Vermes and M. D. Goodman (eds.), *The Essenes According to the Classical Sources* (Oxford Centre Textbooks 1; Sheffield, UK: JSOT Press, 1989).

5. See further F. M. Cross, *The Ancient Library of Qumran* (3d ed.; Minneapolis: Fortress, 1958), 104–5.

6. See S. Iwry, "Was There a Migration to Damascus? The Problem of *šby yśr'l*," in *W. F. Albright Volume* (Erlsr 9; Jerusalem: Israel Exploration Society, 1969), 80–88.

7. See J. Murphy-O'Connor, "The Essenes and Their History," *RB* 81 (1974): 215–44.

8. Murphy-O'Connor, "The Essenes," 222. Cf. W. F. Albright, *From the Stone Age to Christianity: Monotheism and the Historical Process* (2d ed.; Garden City, NY: Doubleday, 1957), 376: "It seems probable that the Essenes represent a sectarian Jewish group which had migrated from Mesopotamia to Palestine after the victory of the Maccabees."

9. See J. T. Milik, *Ten Years of Discovery in the Wilderness of Judaea* (SBT 26; Naperville, IL: Allenson, 1959), 93; J. Magness, *The Archaeology of Qumran and the Dead Sea Scrolls* (Grand Rapids: Eerdmans, 2002), 66–67.

10. See M. Burrows et al. (eds.), *The Dead Sea Scrolls of St Mark's Monastery*, vol. 2, fascicle 2 (New Haven, CT: American Schools of Oriental Research, 1951). For the fragmentary copies of the rule from Cave 4, see P. Alexander and G. Vermes, *Qumran Cave 4, XIX: Serekh Ha-Yaḥad and Two Related Texts* (DJD 26; Oxford: Clarendon, 1998); for the fragmentary copies of the rule from Cave 5, see J. T. Milik in *Les 'Petites Grottes' de Qumrân* (ed. M. Baillet et al.; DJD 3; Oxford: Clarendon, 1962), 180–83.

11. See J. Murphy-O'Connor, "La genèse littéraire de la Règle de la Communauté," *RB* 76 (1969): 528–49; J. Pouilly, *La règle de la communauté de Qumrân: Son évolution littéraire* (Cahiers de la *RB* 17; Paris: Gabalda, 1976).

12. See J. T. Milik in *Qumran Cave I* (ed. D. Barthélemy and J. T. Milik; DJD 1; Oxford: Clarendon, 1955), 107–30.

13. See S. Schechter, *Documents of Jewish Sectaries: Volume I, Fragments of a Zadokite Work* (Cambridge, UK: University Press, 1910); repr. with a prolegomenon by J. A. Fitzmyer (New York:

Ktav, 1970). The lack of adequate photographs of the manuscripts in the Schechter edition has been remedied by M. Broshi, *The Damascus Document Reconsidered* (Jerusalem: Israel Exploration Society and Shrine of the Book, Israel Museum, 1992). This publication contains two important essays; one by J. M. Baumgarten, "The Laws of the Damascus Document in Current Research," pp. 51–62; and the other by F. García Martínez, "Damascus Document: A Bibliography of Studies 1970–1989," pp. 63–83.

14. See J. M. Baumgarten, *Qumran Cave 4, XIII: The Damascus Document (4Q266–273)* (DJD 18; Oxford: Clarendon, 1996).

15. See M. Baillet, J. T. Milik, and R. de Vaux (eds.), *Les 'Petites Grottes' de Qumrân*, 128–31, 181.

IV. The Languages of the Scrolls

1. See E. Qimron, *The Hebrew of the Dead Sea Scrolls* (Harvard Semitic Studies 29; Atlanta: Scholars Press, 1986).

2. The Babylonian Talmud (*b. Shabbat* 115a) contains the report: "It happened once that my father visited R. Gamaliel Berabbi at Tiberias and found him sitting at a table…with the targum of Job in his hands, which he was reading. Said he to him, 'I remember that R. Gamaliel, your grandfather, was standing on a pinnacle of the Temple, when the book of Job in a targumic translation was brought to him. Immediately he said to the builder, "Bury it under the bricks." He [R. Gamaliel II] also gave orders, and they concealed it.'"

V. The Scriptures in the Scrolls: Old Testament, Targums, Canon

1. See I. Ben-Zvi, "The Codex of Ben Asher," *Textus* 1 (1960): 1–16.

2. Apart from an occasional use of it for the Tetragrammaton, *YHWH* (e.g., 1QpHab 10:14; 11:10).

3. See J. A. Sanders, *The Psalms Scroll of Qumrân Cave 11* (DJD 4; Oxford: Clarendon, 1965), 79–85.

4. See Y. Yadin, *The Ben Sira Scroll from Masada* (Jerusalem: Israel Exploration Society and the Shrine of the Book, 1965).

5. See J. A. Fitzmyer, "196–200...," in *Qumran Cave 4, XIV: Parabiblical Texts Part 2* (ed. M. Broshi et al.; DJD 19; Oxford: Clarendon, 1995), 1–76.

6. See J. T. Milik in *Qumrân Grotte 4, II: I. Archéologie. II. Tefillin Mezuzot et Targums (4Q128–4Q157)* (ed. R. de Vaux et J. T. Milik; DJD 6; Oxford: Clarendon, 1977), 48–79. On phylacteries, see *Letter of Aristeas* §159; Josephus, *Ant.* 4.8.13 §213.

7. The passages prescribed for later rabbinic phylacteries differ somewhat from the Essene type, having rather Exod 13:1–10 (unleavened bread at Passover); Exod 13:11–16 (law of the first-born); Deut 6:4–9 (the Shema'); Deut 11:13–21 (promise of bountiful harvest). This type is found in a phylactery from Murabba'at (Mur 4 [see DJD 2. 80–85]).

8. See J. T. Milik in *Qumrân Grotte 4: II* (DJD 6), 80–85.

9. See further E. Tov, *Textual Criticism of the Hebrew Bible* (Minneapolis: Augsburg Fortress, 1992), 100–117.

10. See F. M. Cross in *Qumran Cave 4, VII: Genesis to Numbers* (ed. E. Ulrich et al.; DJD 12; Oxford: Clarendon, 1994), 79–95.

11. See P. W. Skehan and E. Ulrich in *Qumran Cave 4, IX: Deuteronomy, Joshua, Judges, Kings* (ed. E. Ulrich et al.; DJD 14; Oxford: Clarendon, 1995), 137–42.

12. See also Matt 7:12; 11:13 (inverted); 22:40; John 1:45; Acts 22:26.

13. A form of the phrase is found also in Philo of Alexandria, *De vita contemplativa* 3 §25: "Laws and Oracles pronounced by Prophets and Psalms and the rest." Cf. Josephus, *Ag.Ap.*1.1.8 §§39–41, who is aware of the same tripartite division of the OT but does not use a succinct formula to express it.

14. For David as a "prophet," see Acts 2:30–31 ("Because he was a prophet and knew that God had sworn an oath to him that He would set one of his descendants upon his throne, he foresaw and spoke of the Messiah" [alluding to Ps 132:11]). Cf. *Epistle of Barnabas* 12:10 (where Ps 110:1 is introduced by "David himself

prophesies"); J. A. Fitzmyer, "David, 'Being Therefore a Prophet' (Acts 2:30)," *CBQ* 34 (1972): 332–39.

VI. The Use and Interpretation of Scripture in the Sect

1. See B. M. Metzger, "The Formulas Introducing Quotations of Scripture in the N. T. and the Mishnah," *JBL* 70 (1951): 297–307.

2. See also Sir 44:16 ("Enoch pleased the LORD, and he was taken up"); 49:14 ("No one like Enoch was created on earth, for he was taken up from the earth"); Heb 11:5 ("By faith Enoch was taken up so that he would not see death; and he was not found, because God had taken him").

3. See Y. Yadin, *The Temple Scroll* (3 vols. with Supplement; Jerusalem: Israel Exploration Society, 1983).

4. See E. Qimron and J. Strugnell, "4Q394 3–9," in *Qumran Cave 4, V: Miqṣat Ma'aśe ha-Torah* (ed. E. Qimron and J. Strugnell; DJD 10; Oxford: Clarendon, 1994), 7–40.

5. J. J. Collins, "The Son of God Text from Qumran," in *From Jesus to John: Essays on Jesus and Christology in Honour of Marinus de Jonge* (ed. M. de Boer; JSNTSup 84; Sheffield, UK: JSOT Press, 1993), 65–82, esp. 66.

VII. Apocryphal, Sapiential, Liturgical, and Eschatological Literature

1. See J. Strugnell and D. J. Harrington, "415. 4QInstruction[a] (*Mûsār lĕMēvîn[a]*)," in *Qumran Cave 4, XXIV: Sapiential Texts Part 2* (ed. J. Strugnell et al.; DJD 34; Oxford: Clarendon, 1999), 41–49.

2. See E. L. Sukenik, *The Dead Sea Scrolls of the Hebrew University* (Jerusalem: Hebrew University and Magnes Press, 1955), 1–19 (+ plates 16–34, 47 [lower]).

3. See Y. Yadin, *The Scroll of the War of the Sons of Light against the Sons of Darkness* (Oxford: Oxford University Press, 1962).

VIII. Beliefs and Practices of the Sect: Dualism, Eschatology, Messianism, Calendar

1. See further J. A. Fitzmyer, *The Dead Sea Scrolls and Christian Origins* (SDSSRL; Grand Rapids: Eerdmans, 2000), 73–110; and idem, *The One Who Is to Come* (Grand Rapids: Eerdmans, 2007), 88–102.

2. The meaning is not clear there, since *māšîăḥ* may refer to patriarchs.

3. See J. T. Milik, *The Books of Enoch: Aramaic Fragments of Qumrân Cave 4* (Oxford: Clarendon, 1976), 150–61.

4. See further M. O. Wise, *Thunder in Gemini and Other Essays on the History, Language, and Literature of Second Temple Palestine* (JSPSup 15; Sheffield, UK: Sheffield Academic Press, 1994), 13–50.

IX. The Scrolls and Christianity: John the Baptist, Jesus of Nazareth, New Testament

1. See S. Sandmel, "Parallelomania," *JBL* 81 (1962):1–13.

2. See B. E. Thiering, *Redating the Teacher of Righteousness* (Australian and New Zealand Studies in Theology and Religion 1; Sydney: Theological Explorations, 1979), 208–14 (the reader of these pages will note how Thiering strives to conclude that "the question [of identification] must be left open"—in spite of all her vigorous argument for the *"prima facie"* identification). Cf. the review of this book by J. Murphy-O'Connor, *RB* 87 (1980): 425–30.

3. See J. O'Callaghan, "¿Papiros neotestamentarios en la cueva 7 de Qumrán?" *Bib* 53 (1972): 91–100; translated into English in *JBL* 91 (1972 supplement): 1–14.

4. O'Callaghan published a summary account in *Los papiros griegos de la cueva 7 de Qumrân* (Madrid: Bibliotheca de Autores Cristianos, 1974).

5. See C. P. Thiede, *The Earliest Gospel Manuscript? The Qumran Papyrus 7Q5 and Its Significance for New Testament Studies* (Exeter, UK: Paternoster, 1992).

X. The Scrolls and the Writings of Paul of Tarsus

1. See further J. A. Fitzmyer, "Paul and the Dead Sea Scrolls," in *The Dead Sea Scrolls after Fifty Years: A Comprehensive Assessment* (2 vols.; ed. P. W. Flint and J. C. VanderKam; Leiden: Brill, 1998–99), 2:599–621.

2. See further Y. Yadin, "Pesher Nahum (4QpNahum) Reconsidered," *IEJ* 21 (1971): 1–12 (+ pl. I).

3. See R. Bultmann, *Theology of the New Testament* (2 vols.; London: SCM, 1952), 1:51.

4. See further J. A. Fitzmyer, "Qumran and the Interpolated Paragraph in 2 Cor 6:14—7:1," *CBQ* 23 (1961): 271–80; reprinted in slightly revised form in *ESBNT*, 205–17.

XI. The Scrolls and Johannine Writings

1. See J. Ashton, *Understanding the Fourth Gospel* (Oxford: Clarendon, 1991), 205.

2. See R. E. Brown, *The Gospel According to John* (AB 29, 29A; Garden City, NY: Doubleday, 1966, 1970); *The Epistles of John* (AB 30; Garden City, NY: Doubleday, 1982).

3. See R. E. Brown, "The Qumran Scrolls and the Johannine Gospel and Epistles," *CBQ* 17 (1955): 403–19, 559–74; reprinted in abridged form in K. Stendahl (ed.), *The Scrolls and the New Testament* (New York: Harper, 1957), 183–207, 282–91.

4. See R. J. Bauckham, "The Qumran Community and the Gospel of John," in *The Dead Sea Scrolls Fifty Years after Their Discovery: Proceedings of the Jerusalem Congress, July 20–25, 1997* (ed. L. H. Schiffman et al.; Jerusalem: Israel Exploration Society/Shrine of the Book, Israel Museum, 2000), 105–15, esp. 105.

5. See further J. A. Fitzmyer, "Qumran Literature and the Johannine Writings," in *Life in Abundance: Studies in John's Gospel in Tribute to Raymond E Brown, S.S.* (ed. J. R. Donahue; Collegeville, MN: Liturgical Press, 2005), 117–33.

6. Many other passages about this Essene messianic expectation in QL could be cited here; see pp. 80–82 above.

7. See further R. Bergmeier, "Glaube als Werk? Die "Werke Gottes' im Damaskusschrift ii, 14–15 und Johannes 6,28–29," *RevQ* 6 (1967–69): 253–60. Bergmeier mentions that the same phrase occurs in 1QS 4:4, but the sense of it there is hardly parallel to the Johannine usage.

8. See J. H. Charlesworth, "Reinterpreting John: How the Dead Sea Scrolls Have Revolutionized Our Understanding of the Gospel of John," *BRev* 9/1 (1993): 18–25, 54.

XII. The Scrolls and Other Christian Writings

1. See further J. A. Fitzmyer, "A Palestinian Collection of Beatitudes," in *The Four Gospels 1992: Festschrift Frans Neirynck* (ed. F. van Segbroeck et al.; BETL 100; Louvain: Peeters/Leuven University Press, 1992), 509–15.

2. See further Y. Yadin, "The Dead Sea Scrolls and the Epistle to the Hebrews," in *Aspects of the Dead Sea Scrolls* (ed. C. Rabin and Y. Yadin; Scripta hierosolymitana 4; Jerusalem: Magnes Press, Hebrew University, 1958), 36–55, esp. 38.

3. See further J. A. Fitzmyer, *The Genesis Apocryphon of Qumran Cave 1 (1Q20): A Commentary* (BibOr 18B; 3d ed.; Rome: Editrice Pontificio Istituto Biblico, 2004), 109, 246–50.

4. See further D. E. Aune, "Qumran and the Book of Revelation," in *The Dead Sea Scrolls after Fifty Years: A Comprehensive Assessment* (2 vols.; ed. P. W. Flint and J. C. VanderKam; Leiden: Brill, 1998–99), 2:622–48; R. Bauckham, "The Apocalypse as a Christian War Scroll," in *The Climax of Prophecy: Studies on the Book of Revelation* (ed. R. Bauckham; Edinburgh: Clark, 1993), 210–37.

XIII. The Copper Scroll

1. See J. T. Milik, "Le rouleau du cuivre provenant de la grotte 3Q (3Q15)," in *Les 'Petites Grottes' de Qumrân* (ed. M. Baillet et al.; DJD 3; Oxford: Clarendon, 1962) 199–302.

2. It was published by Doubleday of Garden City, NY, in 1960, two years before Milik's official version.

3. See J. Jeremias, *The Rediscovery of Bethesda* (Louisville, KY: Southern Baptist Theological Seminary, 1966).

4. See further H. Shanks, *The Copper Scroll and the Search for the Temple Treasure* (Washington, DC: Biblical Archaeology Society, 2007); A. Wolters, *The Copper Scroll: Overview Text and Translation* (Sheffield, UK: Sheffield Academic Press, 1996).

XIV. The End of the Qumran Community

1. See further R. de Vaux, *Archaeology and the Dead Sea Scrolls* (London: Oxford University Press, 1973), 36–37.

INDEX OF MODERN AUTHORS